SHARING THE FAITH WITH YOUR CHILD

• FROM AGE SEVEN to FOURTEEN •

A HANDBOOK FOR CATHOLIC PARENTS

MARY JO PEDERSEN • JOAN BURNEY

ONE LIGUORI DRIVE, LIGUORI, MO 63057-9999

Imprimi Potest:
James Shea, C.SS.R.
Provincial, St. Louis Province
The Redemptorists

Imprimatur:
Monsignor Maurice F. Byrne
Vice Chancellor, Archdiocese of St. Louis

ISBN 0-89243-444-9
Library of Congress Card Number: 92-81360

Scripture selections taken from *The New American Bible with Revised New Testament*, copyright © 1986, by the Confraternity of Christian Doctrine, Washington, D.C., are used by permission. All rights reserved.

Excerpts from *A Family Perspective in Church and Society: A Manual for All Pastoral Leaders*, copyright © 1987, United States Catholic Conference (USCC); *A Century of Social Teaching*, copyright © 1990, (USCC); *Educational Guidance in Human Love*, copyright © 1983, (USCC), are used with permission. All rights reserved.

Material from *A Child's View of Grief*, Alan D. Wolfelt, Ph.D., Director of the Center for Loss and Life Transition, copyright © 1991, is used with permission.

Material from *Should Your Child Be Home Alone?* developed by Family Service of Metro Omaha, copyright © 1991, is used with permission.

To order, call 1-800-325-9521   *www.liguori.org*
Cover design by Chris Sharp

Contents

To the Parents of a Seven-to-Fourteen-Year-Old

From the moment of birth, your child learns about God and experiences God's love through your ordinary, everyday expressions of care. When you feed, clothe, hug, protect, and nurture your child, you teach your child that the world is basically good and that every individual is precious.

In the grade-school years, your child builds upon that basic trust in God, in you, and in self. This book is written to help you continue to share faith in God with your child as he or she moves from childhood into early adolescence.

The information presented here is intended to go beyond teaching religion at home. It is meant to help you recognize the face of God in the joys and challenges of parenting. You will find helpful information on your child's intellectual, moral, and spiritual development as well as practical ideas for nurturing faith at each stage of growth.

We hope this book will support you in the great privilege and awesome responsibility of assisting God in the continuing creation of the unique person your child is becoming.

Mary Jo Pedersen
Joan Burney

AN OVERVIEW

1. Your Greatest Gift

Seven is fun
Always on the run,
Life is never done.

Fourteen is in between
Hardly feels serene,
Never to be seen.

Mary Jo Pedersen

The greatest gift we can share with our children is our faith in a loving God. The security our children feel when they have the safety net of our unconditional love *and* the love of God creates an atmosphere of positive expectations. In this kind of atmosphere, our children develop the courage to achieve their God-given potential.

Sharing our faith in God with our children is also the greatest gift we can give ourselves. It enhances and enriches our own faith. It turns faith experiences, be it Mass or the simple recognition of God's work in the beauty of a sunset, into a joyous sharing of God's love.

Sharing the Good News of a loving God may sometimes seem an overwhelming task, albeit a joyous one. Yet, it doesn't seem quite as overwhelming when we realize that we are sharing faith in God simply by being a loving parent. It becomes even easier if we have realistic expectations, patience, and a knowledge of the developmental stages our children are experiencing.

Respecting our children's individuality is an important step in creating an atmosphere of faith. Children go through the stages of development at their own individual pace. Some children come into the world smiling and settle down in a spirit of mutual love.

Some are shy. Some are boisterous. Some are born red-faced and angry, determined to challenge the status quo at every turn.

There is a certain predictability, however, about these stages. Experts in the field have developed road maps for parents so they can recognize the various developmental stages and help their children work through them. This knowledge gives us an added edge of understanding when we find ourselves perplexed and wondering, *Whatever happened to my nice, cheerful little child?* This knowledge is detailed in a later chapter.

We also need to evaluate our own skills with reasonable expectations. As much as we love our children, we will not be perfect parents. Perfection is not a human attribute. As hard as we try, we will not always respond with love and wisdom. However, with the help of God, our co-parent, and a road map from experts in the field, we will succeed in the all-important task of sharing our faith.

Our children will not be perfect either — and loving them unconditionally does not mean we will always like what they say or do. Rather, loving unconditionally means that we continue to love our children, even when we don't like what they say or do. This is God's love for us; it is our love for our children. More than anything else, our children need the assurance that we love them when they are least lovable.

Our job is to help our children grow in wisdom, cooperation, courage, and faith. Sometimes this task is frustrating. Children are like fledgling butterflies in a cocoon. We are the cocoon, providing an environment that will nourish their bodies and souls so they can develop wings strong enough to fly. They gain strength in those wings by batting against the walls of that cocoon. Our job is to provide the cocoon; their job is to bat.

The Gift That Lasts

The most important gift we can give our children is the gift of faith. Faith lasts. Children don't grow out of faith or have to replace it. They can take faith with them when they leave home. They can rely on faith to sustain them when they fall and to guide them when they face the pressures of success.

However, we cannot give our children faith like we give them a doll or a bicycle. We can only share it, passing it on to them as we keep it for ourselves. After all, the more faith we share with our children, the more faith we know ourselves.

Many of us, however, don't feel prepared to share faith with our children. We're not sure about what we want to pass on — or should pass on. When children ask questions about heaven, hell, miracles, or the Trinity, how do we know we're giving the right answers? We may be baptized Catholics but not schooled in the rich Catholic traditions. We may be converts who never had matters thoroughly explained to us. Our adult explanations may not seem to fit our child's questions.

As your child enters grade school, you may consider putting him or her in a preparation class for first confession and first holy Communion. Perhaps, however, you are carrying memories of experiences that have left you in some doubt about your own commitment to the Catholic Church. Perhaps you've been negligent of your own faith development because of the pressures of everyday life. Or perhaps you've left the Church because of a divorce or some other reason and are coming back for your child's first Communion. For any number of reasons, you may feel estranged from the Catholic community.

Take heart. Whether you realize it or not, you are already sharing faith with your child. Loving and caring for your child is the first step in sharing faith. Being committed to your family, spending time together, showing appreciation, and making efforts at good communication are all traits of healthy families that help create an environment for faith to grow.

Single parents have the additional challenge of meeting children's needs with little or no support from a spouse. Nurturing faith may seem like a luxury under the circumstances. Still, single parents have a deeply felt need to share the Catholic faith, and that alone will make it possible.

This desire to share your faith is your greatest gift.

A Sense of Humor

The ability to see in a rebellious preteen the fine adult he or she will someday become is enhanced immeasurably by the understanding of this sometimes difficult stage. It also helps to recall how we felt and acted at that age. This may provide the tinge of humor necessary for us to pull back from a potentially explosive situation and handle it in a firm and friendly manner.

One of the best and toughest teachers in Holy Trinity parish in Hartington, Nebraska, is Sister Rose Abeyta. "How do I put up with students who are going through a difficult stage? It's easy — because I've seen the most 'difficult' of my students become our finest citizens. I recognize their potential, and I keep my sense of humor. I don't just expect miracles, I count on them."

Just What Does a Child Need?

As our children progress from age seven to fourteen, their own unique personalities continue to take shape and be shaped by influences outside as well as inside the home. We become increasingly aware of the needs of each child: larger shoes, longer pants, taller bikes, sports equipment, rides to everywhere, haircuts, physical examinations, braces, and curling irons.

We begin to feel the sharp tension between what *we* think are necessities and what the *child* thinks are necessities. Overall, we want our children to be happy. We want to meet their needs — and some of their wants as well. At times, however, it will be difficult to distinguish between wants and needs.

Along with material and physical needs, children have emotional, psychological, and spiritual needs as well. They need to see themselves as good and capable. They need approval, security, affection, and a sense of belonging. In fact, there are so many needs and so many wants that it is easy to become confused: *Just what is a "good" parent to do?*

The First Step

In studies to determine what makes a "healthy" family, experts conclude that having a religious commitment and membership in a faith community are key traits. Of course, it is difficult, if not impossible, for children to have faith in a loving God and in themselves if their basic physical and emotional needs are not met. Youth shelters and juvenile detention centers are filled with children who do not believe in God, in religion, or in themselves because they never learned to trust others or depend on their care.

Trying to be good parents by building strong family ties is a first step to passing on faith.

Our first and greatest teaching tool is our own faith and the example we set. The "do as I say and not as I do" approach to parenting never works. No influence will be as important as our own example. Our image of God, our habits of prayer, our struggle with difficult questions of good and evil, the way we talk and treat others: this is what children watch and learn and model, each in their own way.

In her book titled *Something More,* Jean Fitzpatrick tells us that nurturing children's spiritual lives is "not the same as teaching kids things." Faith doesn't happen by using certain formulas or following instructions. It is "a process of gentle encouragement and patient waiting." It is important to understand that everyone — everyone — longs for and needs a spiritual connection.

Formal religious education is another helpful element in our children's faith development. Catholic schools and parish religious-education programs offer a structure and an environment for teaching children about God's love and how they can respond to God in their everyday lives. Formal religious education also provides our children faith experiences with others their own age. This becomes increasingly important in the passage from seven to fourteen.

Religious-education programs, however, are designed to assist us, not replace us. No one else — priests, teachers, or friends — can influence the development of religious values in our children as powerfully as we can. A great way to learn or relearn things we've forgotten about our Catholic faith is to volunteer to teach or assist in our parish's school or religious-education program. This is a great way to share in our children's faith formation as well. Parish staff can provide easy-to-use materials for whatever level volunteers choose to teach. One enthusiastic parent volunteer said, "I was reluctant to get involved, but the experience has deepened my own faith and appreciation for Catholic tradition and teaching, and it has helped me communicate with my children about our faith."

Another major factor in our children's faith growth is their experience of family rituals and traditions. Children love to say, "In our family, we always…" and then proceed to tell about family traditions during holiday seasons. Children are naturally attracted to rituals, especially in grade school. In fact, they unconsciously create their own daily rituals for simple things such as getting ready for school or preparing for a soccer game. Two years in a row a family cut down their own Christmas tree. The third year the parents decided to buy a tree. They were reminded by their eight-year-old and ten-year-old that they were "breaking tradition."

Simple traditions and rituals nurture a child's spiritual life without "teaching" facts about religion.

God: Your Co-parent

Responsibility for our children does not rest exclusively in our own hands. Since God is the Author of Life, we have a co-parent to love and guide our children along the way. God cherishes and loves our children as much — and more — than we do. Although we create the environment, speak the words, and show examples of faith, only the power of the Holy Spirit can turn hearts toward God. Jesus promised his presence to his followers until the end of time. That presence in the Eucharist, the Scriptures, and in the hearts of all believers is a guarantee that we are not alone in the important task of sharing faith. What a comfort!

A rich dimension of the Catholic faith is its emphasis on the Spirit's continuing power in the community. The first Christians formed communities to support and care for one another and to keep alive the memory of Jesus' words and actions. We have that same power of community to support us: our families and extended families, our neighbors, our faith communities, and the global human family.

Most of us are concerned about our ability to share a faith that we perceive as imperfect. We all have times of doubt, just as we have moments of conviction and faith in God's love and mercy. The Lord understands our imperfections. Our willingness to grow in faith and share the faith with our children is the important ingredient. By listening to our children's questions and entering into the joys and struggles of their growing up, we will learn much from our children. We will glimpse God as not only our co-parent but also as our own loving Parent. In the ordinary growing pains and accomplishments of everyday life, the sacred is revealed — in laughter and tears, in winning and losing, in birth and death. Having a vibrant, living faith is a journey, never a destination.

Resources

Something More: Nurturing Your Child's Spiritual Growth. Jean Grasso Fitzpatrick, Penguin, New York, 1991.

Spiritual Life of Children, The. Robert Coles, Houghton Mifflin Co., Boston, 1990.

2. Understanding Your Seven-to-Fourteen-Year-Old

Growing as a family is a little like climbing a ladder. Each stage of growth gives you a place to put your foot in moving upward toward maturity. If the tasks of a particular stage are not accomplished, that step of the ladder is shaky or missing, causing family members to step backward or get stuck along the way.

Mary Jo Pedersen

When our child climbs the steps of the school bus for the first full day of school, we're overwhelmed. We can hardly believe this is the same tiny, helpless bundle who turned the household upside down by simply rolling over for the first time or by taking that first, unsteady step alone.

The changes that take place in our children from birth to age seven seem amazing in retrospect — but the years ahead hold just as much wonder and adventure. From the gradual ascent to early childhood, we now move to the roller-coaster ride that characterizes ages seven to fourteen.

The grade-school years are a period of immense physical, intellectual, and emotional growth. From age seven to fourteen, our child will move from concrete to abstract thinking, from family first to friends first, and from blind obedience to new levels of moral responsibility and spiritual growth.

This stage begins with belief in Santa Claus and ends with shopping for bras and athletic supporters. Increasingly, our child's energies will be directed outside the family. The child will learn to deal with challenges according to his or her own way of thinking about self and the world.

In this period of growth, our child continues to show a natural, insatiable desire for knowledge and an incredible capacity for learning. The child's thinking will become gradually more logical (except when hormones interfere) and an ability to think abstractly will improve.

Yet, with all the advances in thinking, our child will not make a complete transition to higher logical thinking during this time; that happens in later adolescence. The child will learn personal strengths and limitations and a perception of the expectations of others. The peer group will become a powerful influence during this time.

Boys will have the task of separating from their mothers and defining for themselves what manhood means. Girls will move from mom-worship, at age seven or eight, to thinking Mom knows absolutely nothing, a not-so-delicate balance of imitation and emancipation.

Where Your Child Is Going

There are distinctive tasks facing our children between the ages of seven and fourteen. They will

- learn intellectual, social, and physical skills
- learn rules and structures outside the family
- learn to disagree with others and still be okay
- learn the consequences of breaking rules
- learn to test ideas and values beyond family
- learn to develop internal controls
- learn to cooperate with others
- learn to identify with the same sex

One moment these children will look and act very grownup — and the next moment they will be children again. By the time they reach fourteen, they should be emerging as separate, independent persons with personal values and enough self-awareness to take responsibility for their own needs, feelings, and behaviors. The stage of full adolescence will build on that potential.

Grade-school children move through generally predictable stages of growth. Experts label these stages early childhood (ages 6,7,8), late childhood (ages 9,10,11), and early adolescence (ages 12,13,14). Many helpful books outline what "normal" behavior is at each of these stages.

We can't let "normal" blind us to our children's individuality, however. Growth takes place sporadically and according to each child's growth meter. There are no firm thresholds marking our child's moving from one stage to another. Just knowing what is generally "normal and expected" for egocentric, contrary, and constantly moving eleven-year-olds, however, is a great comfort to us. Books such as the Gesell Institute's *Your Ten to Fourteen Year Old* can be a big help in understanding children and knowing what to expect. This information goes a long way toward calming our inner guilt-monster when it rears its head and makes us ask, *Now what am I doing wrong?* Helpful books are listed in the resource listing on page 19.

Helpful Hints

A book this size does not allow for a great deal of depth and detail. Nonetheless, the following general reminders will help make the changes and challenges of these years easier for both parent and child.

One stage builds on another. The seven-year-old builds on skills and information learned as a five- to six-year-old. The child's normal growth may be interrupted at five or six because of sickness, transition, divorce, or death of a significant person. If this happens, the child will have to "go back," so to speak, to do the tasks of that age. This might include asserting a separate identity, learning that behaviors have consequences, or separating fantasy from reality.

In the same way, eleven-year-olds attempt to separate themselves from their parents based on what they've learned during the ages two and a half and six, which are the other two stages when necessary tasks of separation are learned.

Moving from stage to stage is scary and uncomfortable. It is also exciting, not unlike when a trapeze artist lets go of one swinging bar hundreds of feet in the air and turns around in midair to reach for a second swinging bar. There is a moment of extreme uncertainty before the hand securely grabs the second bar. That uncertainty is the moment of "transition," being in-between two places, not being in either. Experts in human growth call this experience "disequilibrium," which means being off balance. They compare it to periods of "equilibrium," that is, when a child has arrived at a new skill or understanding and is comfortable with it.

Between seven and fourteen years of age, the child will swing from stage to stage. Some days may feel like an actual circus act — especially if there are several children in that age group in the family.

At ten, the child may love life and family, be happy and agreeable most of the time, enjoy being helpful, and be mostly accepting of others. At eleven, this very same child will probably turn contrary, uncooperative, self-absorbed, and quarrelsome.

Again at age twelve, calm may return along with a new tolerance for the differences of others and respect for their feelings. There may be a period of idealism about self and even sincere sympathy for others. If eleven is searching for self, twelve seems to have found it — temporarily, that is.

At thirteen, the outgoing, energetic child will likely turn inward, as he or she did at ages three and a half and at seven. When children turn thirteen, they sometimes withdraw, become noncommunicative, and feel terribly insecure. The thirteen-year-old may appear to live in his or her room, not the house.

This does not mean that every other year between seven and fourteen will be miserable. There is a predictable pattern of disequilibrium and equilibrium that children experience as they work through one stage and go on to the next. Understanding this and making good use of God's wondrous gifts of faith, humor, and patience will help us survive — and even thrive — during these sometimes turbulent years. We can actually understand — and enjoy — our family circus.

Every child has a personal growth meter and proceeds at his or her own pace. Sometimes we worry when our eight-year-old still believes in the Easter bunny or our fourteen-year-old hasn't started menstruating. Information on stages of children's development compiled by child experts is meant to be only a guide. Each child will move through these stages in a unique way, at a pace that is just right for that child. It helps, however, if we understand that there are stages when it is good to encourage certain skills and stages when certain behaviors might be expected.

Faith Development During These Years

As our children move from seven to fourteen, they gain a more mature understanding of God. They begin to understand the many gifts God has given them to use for the good of others. Their appreciation for the importance of Jesus Christ as a life companion deepens. They begin to understand the questions surrounding good and evil.

As they mature, our children will ask disturbing questions about pain and sickness, human and natural catastrophes, and death. Their moral and spiritual development will be strongly influenced by the way we respond or don't respond to their difficult questions. The response (not necessarily the answer) we give to our four-year-old about terminal illness of a loved one will be different from the response we give our fourteen-year-old. Being familiar with the stages of development our children are experiencing gives us reassurance along the way. It helps us fashion more reasonable expectations for each child at each age. How good for the child! How good for us!

Your Child's Capacity to Choose

Between seven and fourteen, children develop the important capacity to choose, along with forming a Christian conscience as a guide. Loving unconditionally can become frustrating at times as our children mature and begin to make independent choices. Yet, the power of free will is God's gift to the human creature — the gift that makes human nature distinctly unique. This full human freedom does not include blind or fearful allegiance to God or to religious or parental authority. Exploring options and making choices during these years enable our children to develop a deeper awareness and knowledge of God, a love of self and others, and a capacity to choose behavior according to personal perceptions.

Our task becomes one of encouragement. We must help our children form decision-making skills; we must foster an environment in which our children can develop responsibility, courage, and faith. Then, in that environment, God's love and a full human response to that love can be learned.

Resources

Moral Development: A Guide to Piaget and Kohlberg. Ronald Duska and Mariellen Whelan, Paulist Press, Mahwah, NJ, 1975.

Stages of Faith: The Psychology of Human Development and the Quest for Meaning. James W. Fowler, Harper San Francisco, San Francisco, 1981.

Your Ten to Fourteen Year Old (rev. ed.). Louis B. Ames, et al., Dell Books, New York, Gesell Institute of Human Development, 1988.

3. The Meaning and Purpose of Faith

Faith, classically understood, is not a separate dimension of life, a compartmentalized specialty. Faith is an orientation of the total person, giving purpose and goal to one's hopes and strivings, thoughts and actions.

James W. Fowler
Stages of Faith

A human being is the only one of God's creatures who asks, "Who am I? Why am I here? What is the meaning of life?" In his book *The Structure of Evil,* Ernest Becker calls men, women, and children "meaning makers."

Unlike other creatures who learn survival from instinct or conditioning, human beings learn by asking questions. Our happiness is not attained from simply having enough to eat and drink, from being bigger or better than others, or having material goods and status. Purpose and meaning are the essence of happiness for human beings.

To find purpose and meaning, a person must have faith. In Alcoholics Anonymous, for example, people turn from harmful addictions because they make the connection with their spiritual needs and their Higher Power. In much the same way, our Catholic religious traditions lead us to a community of faithful who support us in our quest for answers, who provide answers to some of our questions, and who comfort us when we realize that some questions have no answers and some mysteries remain veiled.

Sharing Faith: What Does It Mean?

"Believing without proof" or "a religion or system of beliefs" is usually the first dictionary entry for "faith." But these definitions can be misleading and simplistic. If sharing faith is simply a matter of passing on a set of beliefs or religious practices accepted without proof, we can give our children a book to read or send them off to religion class to learn from the "pros."

The original meaning of the Hebrew word for faith, as used by the early followers of Jesus, meant "alignment of the heart and will," a "commitment of loyalty and trust." The Hebrew, Greek, and Latin words for faith are similar. Its primary meaning from classical Latin *(credo)* is "to entrust, to commit, to trust someone or something." In fact, the word *credo* comes from two Latin words that mean "heart" and "give." In early Christian baptism, catechumens committed themselves — "gave their hearts" — to Christ. By the eighteenth century, however, the secular use of the word *faith* began to change its meaning to "a set of beliefs" that a particular group held in common. The word lost its original focus on trust and commitment to Christ.

Wilfred Smith, an expert in children's faith development, suggests that to be a person of faith today we need to ask "On what or whom do I set my heart?" as well as "What do I believe?" Smith says that faith is basically relational. There is always another person(s) in whom we trust or to whom we are loyal.

The experience of faith begins at birth with the loving and care-filled attention we provide our children. Our children experience the world as a dependable place ("Someone feeds me, holds me, and keeps me comfortable") and begin to "have" faith long before grasping religious concepts.

The Difference Between Faith and Religion

Faith and religion are not separate parts of our children's lives. The two are interdependent. Faith is nurtured and renewed by elements of religious belief and practice. In his book *Faith and Belief,* Wilfred Smith explains faith as "an orientation of the personality, how one sees and treats oneself, one's neighbor, and the universe."

Faith is a quality of human persons. It involves the head, the heart, and the will. Fostering faith in our children means addressing what they think, how they feel, and what they do.

Religion, on the other hand, is an ongoing tradition that celebrates a people's relationship with the Divine. Religion is made up of beliefs, rules of conduct, and rituals. It may have its own literature, symbols, saints, models of holiness, music, and hierarchy. Religion feeds and directs our children's faith in the Divine, in themselves, and in the world.

Religious traditions, like the Catholic Church, communicate beliefs and rituals that bring people together in their search for meaning. Devout Presbyterians, Seventh-Day Adventists, Baptists, Hindus, and Moslems all have faith. Each expresses that faith and is nurtured in it in a different religious tradition.

The Rich Catholic Tradition

The Catholic faith is rooted in a long and rich tradition that includes Church teaching, doctrine, rituals, and a people with a mutual history. Bringing children up in the Catholic faith means exposing them to this fruitful legacy. Catholics enjoy the benefits of a rich sacramental life through which faith is nurtured from the moment of baptism, throughout life, to the Mass of Resurrection. Eucharist is available daily, not as a reward for the just but as food for the hungry and a means of deepening and sustaining faith in Jesus Christ.

Catholics hold in common a salvation history — a family album, so to speak — of God's faithful care over the long haul. Catholics are members of a universal Church whose task it is to carry the Good News to the ends of the earth. The Church's structures are intended to guarantee the integrity and unity of the faithful's unique traditions.

At the heart of the Catholic tradition is each person's commitment to Christ within the believing community. Doctrines, teachings, and traditions are formative tools that help us stay in relationship with God. Individual faith response to all matters of faith varies from person to person. As adult Catholics, our failure to understand or agree with a specific Church teaching does not mean we do not adhere to the Catholic faith. Faith goes beyond blind belief; it includes the mature use of a well-formed conscience and a continuing commitment to follow Christ.

Cradle Catholics (ones who are Catholic from birth) tend to take much of their Catholic tradition for granted. Converts to Catholicism who study and observe it as adults, however, often have a better sense of the uniqueness of the Catholic faith.

Dimensions of Faith

Faith consists of *trusting* in a loving God. Our children can trust God because they've been able to trust us — and others — in small ways. They trust that they will be taken care of, protected, and loved.

Faith consists of *believing*. Believing is a cognitive skill that children develop slowly. Therefore, what our children are able to believe at seven years of age will be different from what they believe at fourteen — and at thirty-four. This believing will influence their actions and attitudes throughout life.

Faith consists of *doing*. Faith propels the believer to action. Our children's decisions about how to act and how to treat others will not always accurately reflect what they believe, however. Their development takes time and their ability to make connections between belief and practice continues to evolve even during their adult years.

Stages of Faith

Sharing faith with our children is like keeping up with yard work; it's a task that is never finished. Just when we think everything is in order and complete, some new growth appears or the season changes and we're into a whole new challenge.

Experts have spent years studying faith development in children and adults. They have found that persons move through somewhat predictable stages of faith growth that parallel the growth of cognitive and social skills. According to Dr. James Fowler, known for his research in the psychology of religion, children move through two or three levels of faith by the time they reach early adolescence. Many people stop at stage three or four; some never make it past stage one. Growing in faith is a lifelong task, and very few reach the final stages. The following summaries help us understand our children's faith potential — as well as our own.

Infancy and undifferentiated faith: This is a "prestage"; it can't really be called a "level." It is a human experience that cannot be studied; yet, it's a prerequisite for human growth. It begins in the womb and continues in infancy. It requires no language for expression and enables a child to overcome the basic anxiety of separation from others. By being fed, changed, cuddled, smiled at, and talked to, children learn to trust in their own worth and in the good of others. This level of faith involves a totally emotional orientation of trust in the world as good and dependable. Nurturing is critical during this stage.

Intuitive-projective faith (level one): This first level of faith emerges in early childhood along with the use of language (somewhere between two and six years of age). Stimulated through stories, symbols, and gestures, images of God and truth are created in the young imagination. Exposure to positive images of God and the world through stories and lived experiences are important. Our own image of God will strongly affect our children at this stage. To children at this level of faith development, the Bible is simply a series of separate, unconnected stories about people and events that happened long ago. There is a great curiosity and interest in spectacular events and people such as floods, fires, and persons who perform outstanding feats. A growing curiosity about what is real and what is fantasy will propel children to the next stage of faith.

Mythic-literal faith (level two): At this level of faith, children develop concrete operational thinking: the ability to think logically. At this level, faith emerges somewhere around the first to third grade. Children begin to buy into a belief system that helps them bring order to the expanding world around them, provided the belief system is presented by believable, trusted adults. God is seen in concrete human form. Images of the Good Shepherd, an old man with a beard, and the King of the Universe help children at this level understand who God is. The Bible is a book of connected stories about God; an interest in what is literally true (and not just a story) increases at this level. Children will ask a lot of questions — questions that will lead them to the next and more mature stage of faith.

Synthetic-conventional faith (level three): The physical and emotional changes of puberty create tremendous potential for this next stage of faith growth. Sometime in early adolescence our children begin to experience emotional solidarity with others. Special friends are usually our children's first experience of intimacy outside the family. Belief in a personal, loving God and a set of principles can develop as a means of bringing order and structure to the increasing number of influences affecting our children in these years. Their image of God becomes more personal at this level and is identified with abstract personal qualities like a compassionate friend or a strict scorekeeper. Children can begin to break sexual stereotypes of God at this stage and to see both masculine and feminine attributes in their personal image of God, if both are presented.

The term *conventional faith* hints at the child's tendency to conform to expectations and beliefs of significant others. Though our children may externally resist our religious traditions at the age of eleven or twelve, internally they want a belief system to which they can conform. This system helps them form a sense of self-definition and gives them a limit to press against in their efforts at emancipation. (They need to strengthen their wings.)

Many persons get "stuck" at this stage because they are completely dependent upon the expectations and evaluations of others; they cannot critically reflect on their faith and make it their own. This critical reflection and internalization of faith come in the next stage and begin generally in late adolescence and early adulthood. When a child leaves home or is introduced to alternative value systems and beliefs held by people he or she trusts, the opportunity to move to the next individuating-reflective stage is presented.

Later stages of faith development: The next three stages of faith development usually occur in late adolescence and adulthood. In these stages, persons begin to "own" their faith in a personal loving God and accept responsibility for acting according to their beliefs.

In stages four and five, adults learn to live more peacefully with the paradoxes of life and eventually recognize the truth in faith traditions other than their own.

The deeper one grows in faith, the more consistent beliefs and actions become and the less egocentric a person is. These growth stages take time and an environment of spiritual nurturing. Many adults find faith "mentors" to be helpful along the way.

Many people let years go by without movement. Then their child's first Communion or questions about God will stimulate their spiritual growth. For some, the death of a parent or friend, a child's sickness or handicap, or some other traumatic event may precipitate a crisis of faith that leads to growth.

Your Role as Parent

Perhaps we feel that our trust in a loving God, our belief in the Church's teachings, or our everyday actions do not model a mature faith for our children. We may feel that our own faith is not strong enough to be a spiritual force at home. Because we're not certain how deep our own faith is, we may feel inadequate to nurture our children's faith growth. Our response to God's invitation to love is slow, and sometimes it's one step forward and two steps back.

Looking at faith from another perspective may help. Faith is not only a human dynamic and response; faith is also a free gift from God. God made a covenant with us to love us without condition. An invitation to respond in love was initiated by God — and is constantly repeated by God throughout history. Faith is not something we, as parents, discovered or invented. The Catholic faith was passed on to us from others, given to us by parents, grandparents, friends, priests, nuns, and countless saints along the way. For centuries, the gift has been passed from generation to generation, from parish to parish, from nation to nation.

In his book *Pass It On,* Father James Ewens explains that parents educate their children about religion by being parents. The primary content of this education is expressed most clearly in routine, day-to-day family life.

Our children's faith is God's gift to them. As parents, it's our privilege and responsibility to be a part of passing on this gift by simply being the best parents we know how to be, day in and day out. In this way, we share our gift of faith — and we receive a greater measure of the gift for ourselves.

Resources

Discovering: A Junior High Religion Program. Michael Carotta, Thomas Zanzig, ed., St. Mary Press, Winona, MN, 1989.

Faith and Belief. Wilfred C. Smith, Princeton University Press, Princeton, NJ, 1987.

Structure of Evil, The. Ernest Becker, Free Press, New York, 1976.

Will Our Children Have Faith? John H. Westerhoff, Harper San Francisco, San Francisco, 1983.

HUMAN DEVELOPMENT AND THE FAITH JOURNEY

1. The Beginning of the Journey

Faith is a journey, never a destination.
Joan Burney

Exterior changes in children between the ages of seven and fourteen are evident. They grow out of clothes, take up more room in the car, and appear notably taller in family pictures. Interior changes are just as dramatic and important. Our children begin to reason logically, see how they fit into society, make moral decisions about behavior, and believe in God and in themselves.

Just as their physical growth takes place in generally predictable stages, so too does their cognitive, moral, social, and faith growth. In this section, we will trace some aspects of our children's development that will help us in our efforts to share our faith.

The grade-school years are often divided into the primary, intermediate, and junior-high years. Remember, children proceed physically and mentally at their own pace. Some are six feet tall in the eighth grade while others are only four feet ten inches. In the same way, interior growth, although it follows predictable stages, is different with each child and must be respected. Some children may sail through the stages with little difficulty; others will struggle. Although some stages may seem easier to deal with than others, don't view one stage as being better or easier than another.

It's all movement that is crucial to children's growth toward maturity.

The following summaries describe the characteristics of each stage of development and suggest ways to nurture faith at that particular stage.

2. First Grade Through Third Grade

Running down the staircase
Legs are getting long
Teeth in front are MIA.
Where's my baby gone?

In primary grades, a whole new world opens to a growing child. In first grade, the world still centers on self and home. By third grade, however, relationships and the broader outside world become more significant.

General Description

Before they enter first grade, children will think in a prelogical and magical way. They will be satisfied with magical explanations of what and why things are the way they are.

By the end of the primary grades, children will move into the next stage of cognitive development: logical thought. They may still have difficulty separating fact from fantasy and may hold on to some of their own fantasy life. They will, however, gradually acquire more complex abilities. They will begin to understand cause and effect and to reverse a thought process. For example, a child will be able to replay the steps she took to school to find where she left her book bag.

Stories, songs, and hands-on activities are good ways to share faith with children at the primary stage. In her work with children's faith development, Mary Wilcox discourages parents from explaining the religious significance of a story, the concept they should learn, or the meaning of words in a song. For children in this age group, songs, games, and stories are the lesson. Pressuring children into complex explanations is nonproductive; they simply do not understand. It may turn them off to seeking such information in the future when it's more age-appropriate.

As in most stages of growth, the love and care we display for our children at this age will be their strongest "proof" of the existence of a loving God. Our children will celebrate the sacraments of reconciliation and first holy Communion during this time. Our own active participation in their preparation will allow us many opportunities to nurture the gift of faith in them, in ourselves, and in our entire family. In our children's sacramental preparation classes, we will be given helpful suggestions for our family's celebration of these important faith moments. Belonging to a Catholic faith community in which others hold similar beliefs and traditions reinforces children's faith. This is especially important in this period when children begin to recognize their own family as different from other families in the larger world.

As their world broadens to include school, church, and neighborhood, children move from obeying those who are more powerful toward a willingness to cooperate with others who can be of use to them. Their obedience is based more on a hope for reward than on fear of punishment. A hug or a word of appreciation is a powerful reinforcing tool at this time.

It is crucial for us to provide children in this age group with a cause-and-effect understanding of discipline. An important part of our children's ability to respect faith will rest on the respect our children have for us — and the respect we have for ourselves. That respect is built, in part, on effective discipline. If you haven't had much luck at discipline up to this point, you may want to avail yourselves of books or parenting classes that will help you learn ways to be more effective. It is never too late.

It is appropriate to discuss differences of opinion with your children, and sometimes compromise. Open discussions and compromises teach your children the value of give-and-take. Regarding matters of your children's physical well-being, moral formation, and faith development, of course, you must stand firm. Children respect this. In fact, despite their anger, children get the much-needed message "My parents love me enough to insist I do what they think is best for me." It is in this atmosphere of mutual respect that faith thrives.

Though children at this stage still see themselves as the center of the world, they begin to see the significance of other relationships. Fortunately, they will continue to be egocentric in decreasing degrees through adolescence. Relationships with others become gratifying and more important as they mature.

The primary-school child develops a new skill that is especially important for religious formation and faith development: the ability to think symbolically. Before this stage, children see symbols as identical to what they represent. The Bible, for instance, is a book of stories. At this stage, however, they begin to understand that symbols represent something else, something deeper, something more than the concrete object in front of them. They cannot yet understand the Bible as the Word of God, but they can begin to appreciate the people, events, and human realities portrayed in the stories.

At this developmental stage, children will increasingly be able to find practical ideas from observation. They begin to predict probable patterns that will lead them to a more orderly view of their world. As children grow in these cognitive abilities, their faith moves toward what is called "affiliative faith": "No longer *my* faith but *our* faith, the faith of my family and my church community."

Formal Religious Education

In the primary grades, children learn about the Church as the family of God and as a sign of Jesus' presence in the world. They are introduced to Jesus as redeemer, brother, and friend. They learn about God, who is creator, and the Holy Spirit, who continually guides and gifts every person and the Church as a whole. They learn about Mary, the Mother of God, who is also our mother. She is presented as an example of saying yes to God's will.

The sacraments are presented as signs of the welcoming, nourishing, and forgiving love of God. Children who are welcomed with open arms develop a special relationship with their faith. Emphasis is placed on the sacrament of reconciliation and first holy Communion.

Most Catholic parishes provide some religious-formation programs for children. The teacher's task is to assist us, the primary religious educators, in our efforts to pass on the faith to our children. Religious-education programs vary to some degree from parish to parish.

Getting to know our children's teachers and examining the educational material are good ways to learn about and reinforce our children's religious education. This information allows us to support at home what is learned in school. Our attention and interest in what our children are doing in class and in the written material they bring home affirm its importance. Our participation in the primary grades is made easier because of educational opportunities frequently offered to parents of children celebrating reconciliation and first holy Communion. Interfaith families may find these meetings particularly helpful in finding common denominators for sharing their two religious traditions in the home.

Many parishes include children in the planning and participation at special children's liturgies. Children proclaim the Word, design banners, write offertory petitions, and so forth. If your parish doesn't have this opportunity, encourage it — and offer to help.

The resource listing on page 35 contains suggestions for books and material that will be of assistance.

Prayer, Celebration, and Ritual

The following ideas for prayer, celebration, and ritual in the home are ways to celebrate with primary-school children. Draw on your own imagination to develop memorable, personal traditions of prayer and celebration appropriate to your child's development. If you're not imaginative, and many people aren't, religious bookstores have many books that will give you ideas. Several practical, low-cost books of this type are mentioned in the resource listing on page 35.

Develop a habit of evening, morning, and meal prayer. If you don't have this tradition, your child's first Communion is a fitting time to begin. These can be simple, formal prayers or spontaneous ones, whatever you are most comfortable with. Ritual gestures such as lighting a candle, kneeling, holding hands, or singing can be included. The liturgical seasons offer a rich variety of symbols to use in daily prayer.

Children at this age usually feel free to express themselves in prayer in a safe environment free from criticism. Never correct or criticize a child's prayer. Criticism will create self-consciousness and may limit a child's openness to prayer later on. If there's a problem, you may want to make suggestions about what to do differently next time.

Establish simple rituals of reconciliation or forgiveness for you and your child or for the whole family. Say a simple Act of Contrition with your child several nights a week. Memorize the child's prayer used for reconciliation and pray it with your child. Or simply ask God for forgiveness for your failures of the day. When you pray, mention only your own failings; never name or ask forgiveness of God for your child's shortcomings. The main purpose of simple reconciliation is to understand that forgiveness is always granted by a loving God. More detailed rituals of reconciliation with the whole family are found in books about family prayers that are mentioned in the resource listing on page 35.

Bless your child regularly. Our Jewish ancestors had a great tradition of passing on God's blessing to their children. Some modern psychologists claim that children subconsciously seek blessings from their parents. Such blessings affirm and encourage. Tracing a simple sign of the cross on a child's forehead or patting the child's head and saying "God bless you and keep you" is a powerful way to share faith. Encourage a simple response such as "Amen" or "Thank you" as a sign of acceptance. Some families bless one another when departing for long trips, when the children are feeling sick, or when they are entering competitions. This ritual reminds both parent and child of the ever-present availability of God's help. Suggestions for other blessings can be found in the resource listing on the next page.

Keep prayer books available. As early as possible, help your children initiate and lead family prayer. Ask your child to find a prayer in a children's prayer book, a prayer that can be used for the evening meal or just before bed. Though children like to pray spontaneously, some dinner and bedtime hours are so chaotic that choosing a prayer and reading it from a book causes less stress than asking for spontaneous prayers. You will know intuitively what nights or mealtimes to bring out the books for help in praying together.

Display Christian art and symbols in visible places in your home. The home environment makes statements about beliefs and values the family respects. A crucifix or cross, a painted or carved representation of Jesus as Good Shepherd, or a Madonna picture or statue are silent testimonies to what your household believes. These items are not idols or lucky charms; they are sacramentals that serve as reminders to deepen our consciousness of God's presence. There are many lovely representations of Christ with children that may be appropriate in a child's room or in the hallway outside their bedroom doors. Icons and other pictures of a child's name saint are appropriate first Communion gifts, as are children's religious pictures and story Bibles. The Scriptures should be visible in some room in the home, for prayer as well as a reminder of the ongoing presence of Jesus in the Word of God. During Lent and Advent, move the Bible to a table in the living room or kitchen for special seasonal prayer.

Read to your child from good literature. Much good literature provides role models of courage and virtue. In his book *Uses of Enchantment: The Meaning and Importance of Fairy Tales,* Bruno Bettelheim emphasizes the power of a good story to help children deal with their inner fears and fantasies. Religious imagination is a powerful human tool for both children and adults. Children can use the building blocks of virtue, courage, and integrity as portrayed in stories to search for the meaning of life and their own identity.

Resources

Children's Liturgies: Seventy-Four Eucharistic Liturgies, Prayer Services and Penance Services Designed for Primary, Middle, and Junior High Children. Bernadette Kenny, Paulist Press, Mahwah, NJ, 1977.

More Children's Liturgies. Maria Bruck, ed., Paulist Press, Mahwah, NJ, 1981.

Prayer After Nine Rainy Days and Other Family Prayers. Pat C. Hinton, Harper San Francisco, San Francisco, 1978.

Praying With Children: Twenty-Eight Services for Various Occasions. Gwen Costello, Twenty-Third Publications, Mystic, CT, 1990.

Sunday Mass: What Part Do You Play? Robert Rietcheck, C.SS.R., and Daniel Korn, C.SS.R., Liguori Publications, Liguori, MO, 1985.

Uses of Enchantment: The Meaning and Importance of Fairy Tales. Bruno Bettelheim, Knopf, Westminster, MD, 1976.

Your Child's First Communion. A Redemptorist Pastoral Publication, Liguori Publications, Liguori, MO, 1990.

3. Fourth Grade Through Sixth Grade

*Projects, practice, games, and friends
Constant going never ends.
Baths and chores are a bitter pill,
Will my child ever sit still?*

Children who are in fourth, fifth, or sixth grade (the intermediate grade level) continue to expand beyond the home. Peers, school and church activities, and other interests gain a greater hold on these children's enthusiasm. Peer association becomes increasingly more important. As parents, we often begin to feel like we need to make appointments to spend time with our children.

General Description

Children in this age group are active in hobbies, sports, and organizations outside the home. Not all children will begin the process of puberty by the sixth grade. Because the onset of puberty is beginning chronologically earlier than before, we will address its beginning in this section.

When children begin to look grown up, we often expect them to act like adults. Yet, they are not small adults; they are children whose mental processes and ways of approaching the world are considerably different from adults. They will not respond as adults.

Children at this stage think by reasoning about things that are part of their own lived experience. Providing a wide variety of experiences markedly improves their reasoning abilities. Though they can generalize in their thinking and figure out cause and effect more readily than before, they still do not reason with abstractions such as love or justice. Children at this stage still think concretely and need to see things to believe them.

This is a critical time for building self-esteem. Since their self-worth at this stage is determined by their ability to perform tasks and achieve goals set for them, children may keep a mental ledger of all the skills they've mastered and the things they've accomplished. If your child has a handicap or a disability, help the child set reasonable expectations and avoid comparisons that may diminish his or her self-esteem. Support groups are available for children with special needs and for their parents.

Sexual maturation will accelerate by the end of this stage. Girls begin puberty, typically, between ages nine and twelve. Boys begin puberty at a later age, usually around twelve through fourteen. Boy-girl friendships developed in early childhood may dissolve in these intermediate years. Gradual changes in their bodies are accompanied by mixed emotions toward the other sex. They may even regard each other as mean or stupid. Boys will experience growth spurts and unexpected voice changes. Girls will begin menstruating.

Though they are unable to understand a complex moral order, children in fourth, fifth, and sixth grades will see value in "Do unto others…" not for its own sake, but for how it can get their personal needs met. They are obedient to rules and regulations, mostly out of a desire for reward or affirmation. Self-interest and fairness are the guiding rules for friendships and relationships with others.

At this age, children tend to take on the beliefs, stories, and traditions that belong to the community they are closest to. They will interpret stories and actions literally and think somewhat uncritically until they're eleven or twelve years old. Symbols still have great teaching value, though they must refer to something specific. That "something," however, can be an imaginative idea rather than a particular concrete thing.

These children's images of God may be that of rule-maker or judge. Now is the time to expose children to a variety of images of God so their concept can expand appropriate to this faith level. Many adults never pass beyond this stage and are unable to form a mature notion of a compassionate, gracious God in later life.

When we share Scripture with children at this age, we shouldn't offer strict interpretations or correct their one-dimensional views. Their ability to think abstractly is developing gradually. They cannot move to a later stage of development until this stage is completed. Forcing children to give verbal assent to something they cannot understand can retard natural curiosity and questioning — an essential part of the normal process of intellectual and spiritual growth.

Offer children ways of sharing and learning about faith. Children in the intermediate grades make especially good Sunday school and preschool assistants. They're usually happy to visit nursing homes and other institutions and preform countless acts of simple service. Let the children participate in the Sunday liturgy as lectors or greeters. Give them opportunities to choose faith experiences that meet their need for belonging to the larger community. They need to see themselves as contributing members with an important role in the world outside their homes.

Formal Religious Education

Because children begin to think more abstractly at this age, they come to a richer understanding of the meaning behind symbols used in celebrating the sacraments. For this reason, most formal catechetical programs for children in intermediate grades look again at the seven sacraments to bring children to a deeper appreciation of their meaning. The programs focus on the Church as the Body of Christ and emphasize the privileges and responsibilities of membership in it. Children become more familiar with the liturgical calendar of the Church and the way it teaches and celebrates major beliefs of the Catholic faith.

A deeper look at Scripture in these grades emphasizes the history and formation of the inspired Word of God, the Bible, and of salvation history. The curriculum usually includes the story of God's covenant with Israel, the law that flows from that covenant, the Ten Commandments of the Old Law, and the two great commandments of the New Testament.

Children learn more about Jesus as Messiah, fully God and fully human, sent to bring all people to God. They are taught about Christ's presence in the sacraments, the Scriptures, and in other persons. During the fifth or sixth grade, some attention is given to sexuality with the focus on sexuality as a gift from God. This is offered as part of an ongoing sexuality-education program or within the context of the religious-education curriculum, depending on the church or school. More information is available in the section titled "Sexuality" (page 136).

Prayer, Celebration, and Ritual

Sharing the faith with your child takes initiative on your part. The following suggestions encourage faith growth in the home for families with children in the intermediate grades.

Give your child a leadership role in family prayer. At this stage, children enjoy creating, participating, and leading others in prayer. In interfaith families, children can be enriched by choosing prayer forms from both faith traditions. To introduce reflective prayer opportunities, read from Scripture and invite your children to reflect on its meaning. Inspiration for prayer can come from the Church's liturgical calendar as well.

Support your child's tendency to keep count and collect things. Design family celebrations and rituals around this natural interest. Advent and Lent provide opportunities for service or kindnesses that children can take pride in and keep track of.

Celebrate the anniversary of your child's baptism either on the day it occurred or during Holy Week. Display pictures of the ceremony, the baptismal certificate, cards, or baby books. Let your children choose the meal, and present them with a small gift. Include baptism symbols of water, fire, and oil as part of your celebration. One family used the three nights before Holy Thursday to celebrate the baptisms of each of their three children as a preparation for the Easter triduum services that commemorate the baptism of the faithful. This reinforces children's notion of belonging to a community larger than their family. This desire to belong outside the home becomes increasingly important to children in this stage of growth.

Celebrate your child's talents, victories, and accomplishments with rituals and prayers of gratitude. Stop for ice cream after piano recital or a soccer team's victory or offer prayers of thanksgiving to God for a good report card or a completed science project. One family never places a sports trophy on the mantle until it passes through the back doors of the church for a quick prayer of gratitude. These rituals help children recognize that their skills and talents are gifts to be used for God's glory and the service of others. This understanding prepares children for confirmation. It challenges them to recognize the Spirit's influence in their lives as they exercise full membership in the Church.

Take your child to liturgical services celebrating key moments in the lives of others. Children learn through imitation in the intermediate years. To prepare them for the emotional solidarity that is beginning to develop in them, take them to weddings, funerals, baptisms, and first Communions of family and friends.

Their formal religious instruction is reinforced by observing others participating in the sacramental life of the larger community. They may not make clear connections between religious practices and the faith that is being expressed, but the experience itself is formative.

Children's growth is stimulated by rewards at this stage. Affirm and reward your children's spiritual progress, just as you would affirm their progress in academics and sports. An extra story at night or a stop for a doughnut after church tells your children that the maturing of their spirits is as important as the growth and maturing of their bodies. Children may also be commended for reminding the family of night prayers, baking cookies for a sick friend, or going to Mass an extra day during the week.

Resources

Enriching Faith Through Family Celebrations. Sandra DeGidio, Twenty-Third Publications, Mystic, CT, 1989.

Self-Esteem: A Family Affair. Jean I. Clarke, Harper San Francisco, San Francisco, 1985.

4. Seventh Grade Through Ninth Grade

Phone's grown on the earlobe now,
Room's become a private cell.
One-word answers meet my questions.
Is this the child I knew so well?

Confrontation and questioning characterize the junior-high years. The normal and natural task of adolescence is to test limits.

If limits are not tested to some degree — or if there are no limits — children cannot move from adolescence into a more mature stage where limits come from within. When our children are at this stage, we harvest the benefits from the love, mutual respect, and firm discipline of previous years.

General Description

This stage — early adolescence — ushers in an ongoing period of dynamic change for children. The biological upheaval characteristic of this age introduces a period of tremendous growth: physical, moral, intellectual, and social. Whether children are actually experiencing or simply anticipating puberty, their feelings, attitudes, and self-images will be radially affected. Expect growth spurts, bodily changes, new feelings about persons of the other sex, and rapid mood swings. Parents sometimes wonder if this developmental stage is going backward on the inside while raging forward on the outside. Children move through this stage at very different paces.

Though this can be a time of outward bravado and showing off for peers, it is really a time of tremendous self-consciousness. Children at this age struggle to answer "Who am I?" and "What do others think of me?"

By eleven or twelve years of age, many children will be capable of formal, logical thinking. They learn to clarify information, draw conclusions, and interpret data. Using these skills, they begin to construct their own picture of the world as they see it.

At this age, children can act on a set of beliefs and values and speak in defense of them. These beliefs often conform to whatever group the individual values most. Role models have great significance during this period of early adolescence. During this time, it is wise to introduce our children to other adult role models. Teachers, religious educators, clergy and religious, adult neighbors, friends, grandparents, aunts and uncles, and public figures who are examples of Christian living can help us reinforce Christian principles and beliefs.

We may feel like we have little influence on our children's faith growth at this stage. Recent research, however, indicates otherwise. Throughout our children's adolescent years, we remain the primary influence in matters of faith and religion. Our children need our love most when they seem determined to be unlovable.

Children at this age seek approval by doing what's expected of them at the moment. Their self-image is shaped largely by what others think of them. Since there are so many other groups children feel a part of (friends, athletic teams, classmates), they may deal with the conflicting views of themselves by compartmentalizing: by behaving differently in different environments.

The moral reasoning of children at this age is based on this need for approval from those they respect and trust. For the first time, intentions become a consideration in determining an action's moral value. These children will quickly dismiss poor judgment of peers by claiming that they mean well or didn't mean to do it.

At this stage, children begin to understand several levels of meaning for symbols that previously represented concrete objects. They begin to connect abstract concepts to concrete symbols.

The stage of faith children enter into at this age is called a conformist, dependent faith. This is an important and necessary stage children must pass through on their way to a more mature faith commitment. Remember that no one stage of development is good or bad; all stages are necessary for movement and growth toward the next, higher level of functioning.

During this period, children may resist anything they perceive as force-fed religion or indoctrination. They will quickly point out how our actions are inconsistent with our beliefs. Our best response is to admit that we do, indeed, have difficulty being consistent and fair in all our actions. We do well to admit to our imperfections and to point out how children and adults alike are always growing, changing, learning. Children respect and recognize honesty.

Expect confrontation and questioning. Children will think silently to themselves or say openly "I don't believe that because...." Our response to these statements and questions is important in the long-term faith development of our children. Expressing the question out loud is an important step in testing the limits of belief — and remember, testing limits is the adolescent's job. By testing limits, our children learn the importance of setting their own limits.

Statements like "You have to believe" or "Don't talk like that" shut off communication and hinder movement to a deeper level of understanding and acceptance. "I sometimes felt like that, too, when I was your age" and "I understand you're having trouble with this right now" are statements that acknowledge and respect the child's feelings. We have to listen without being judgmental; really listen.

Our willingness to listen and understand will disarm our children's anger. They realize that their confusions are important to us. "I don't know the answer to that, but it's a good question. Let's find somebody who can answer it, and we'll both learn something" conveys to our children that the process of questioning is, in itself, worthwhile. Such statements communicate the unconditional love and acceptance we want our children to experience.

Children at this stage need someone to listen to their questioning. They need freedom to express opinions even if the opinions are contrary to our own beliefs. Their struggle with apparent contradictions and conflicts in the stories and rules they accepted as younger children is a good sign. For example, make what they learn about biological evolution fit with what they learned as young children in the creation stories in Genesis. Our children's doubts and questions are not to be feared or ridiculed; these doubts and questions indicate that the journey toward a more mature faith is underway.

As our children move out of this stage and into the stage of full adolescence, our own actions, choices, and examples in matters of faith will have a greater influence than having answers to questions about morality or religion.

Throughout our children's adolescent years, we will come to depend more and more on the parish or larger Church to assist us in passing on the faith. Because our children are emancipating themselves, other faith-filled environments will play an increasingly important role in their faith development.

Formal Religious Education

Junior-high children learn about the history, mission, and ministry of the Catholic Church. They build on their previous understanding of Church as Christ's presence and as the people of God. They learn about the structure and governance of this complex institution that is itself intended to be a sign of Christ's presence to the world. They are exposed to more facts of Jesus' identity as savior, liberator of the oppressed, and pathway to God. They continue to study the Old Testament in depth, both as literature and inspired Word. They are taught that Mary is called Mother of the Church and is an example of obedience, humility, and faith.

Junior-high students learn that the covenant God entered into with them requires love and service of others. There is an emphasis on formation of conscience rooted in a fundamental set of Christian values and an obligation to live by them. Responsible exercise of free will, skills in decision-making, and accountability for personal actions constitute the principal elements in the catechesis of early adolescents.

Many religious-education programs include preparation for the sacrament of confirmation at this time, although some wait until high school. The formal instruction for this important rite of passage to adult faith includes an appreciation for the role of the Holy Spirit in personal faith life and the life of the Church as a pilgrim people. Children learn about the importance of God's grace available in this and all the sacraments.

Preparation for confirmation requires the cooperation of each child, his or her parents, and the teacher or pastoral staff of the parish. Our involvement will strengthen our children's faith. It will also strengthen our own faith journey and give us an opportunity to return to the sacramental life of the Church if we've been away. The presence of the congregation at confirmation affirms the larger community's duty and privilege to support these children in the process of maturing in their faith.

Prayer, Celebration, and Ritual

At the very time early adolescents need structure, limits, and faith-filled role models, their actions and desires resist our well-meaning efforts. The following ways of passing on the faith at home have worked for many families. They can be adapted for unique circumstances, or they may stimulate further creative ideas.

Move from instruction to invitation in family prayer times. By age twelve, some children will begin to criticize and resist family prayer: "This is weird. This is stupid." They may go so far as to refuse to cooperate. Gently acknowledge your children's feelings and continue to invite them to be a part of prayer. Ask them to assist younger brothers and sisters or to take new roles in participation. One thirteen-year-old boy was asked by his dad to construct three crosses out of scraps of wood for their family's prayer service. When the family gathered for prayer around the crosses, the boy was willing to participate.

If your children resist strongly, give them permission to separate themselves from the family at times of prayer. Let them go to their room or some other part of the house, but without benefit of phone, TV, or music until family prayer is over. Later, you might privately suggest a simple, formal prayer (like the Our Father) or a brief, informal blessing. If you stop praying together because of your children's resistance, you state that prayer is not important and is valued only when everyone enjoys it. Invite your children — all of them — to prayer each time you gather, regardless of what their recent responses to similar invitations may have been.

During this stage, listening to sacred music by popular artists, accompanied by a brief period of silence and a short formal prayer, is far more comfortable than something somber. Such flexible creativity respects the going inward that early adolescents do as part of their normal developmental growth.

Regularly involve the family in service of others. Involve your family in parish activities with other families who have children this age. If there is resistance, acknowledge it but do not punish or reprimand. Offer rewards and affirmations. At this age, your children may feel embarrassed to be with the family in large groups, but there is comfort in knowing that other children their age are suffering the same experience. Children this age usually flock together at functions of this sort — and complain of boredom. However, the experiences of belonging to family and a larger community are of great importance in the children's task of establishing identity.

Become involved in the formal religious education of your child. Some children will not want their parents to be a teacher or visible leader in youth or catechesis. Yet, giving your time in some way will demonstrate the importance you place on faith in action. Providing transportation, chaperoning, or helping with special projects gives witness of your support. If needed, rely on other adults to help mentor your children's religious growth during this period. You, however, continue to be the primary influence in your children's faith development during these years.

Take the sexual education of your child seriously. Sharing religious beliefs, values, and understanding of human sexuality with children will feel awkward to some parents. Many adults bring their own poor sexuality education to their parenting; they never received information directly from their parents about sex and have the impression that their children already "know it all." This you can count on: your children will get plenty of explicit education about sex — from television, music, movies, and the advertising industry. If you remain silent, the media will do this task for you, and the results will not be wholesome or respectful of your children's faith journey.

If you can't explain the Church's teachings on sexuality and have trouble articulating your own beliefs, ask for help. Make a concerted effort to see that your children learn about sexuality from a Catholic perspective. Sexuality instruction and formation should combine the biological facts about sexuality with it's spiritual meaning in God's plan. There are many good books to help you share sexual values and information with your children. In the resource listing below, you will find some helpful suggestions for passing on the Catholic Christian perspective of human sexuality.

Living your faith should not become a power struggle within the family; it should be a mutually shared journey. At this stage, children will try your patience. It's their way of strengthening their wings by batting them against the cocoon of parental concern. Understanding the turmoil of these years, praying for patience, and viewing your children with faith and humor will help keep things in perspective. Stand firm on matters that physically, mentally, or morally threaten your children. In issues that aren't life-threatening or morally threatening, allow your children to make their own choices. Provide them with roots of faith in a loving God; allow them to become increasingly independent. When the time comes for them to leave home, their wings will be strong enough to fly.

Resources

Book of Family Prayer, Gabe Huck, Harper San Francisco, San Francisco, 1984.

Forgiving Family: First Step to Reconciliation. Carol Luebering, St. Anthony Messenger Press, Cincinnati, 1983.

Power of a Parent's Words: How You Can Use Loving, Effective Communication to Increase Your Child's Self-Esteem and Reduce the Frustrations of Parenting. H. Norman Wright, edited by Ed Steward, Regal Books, Ventura, CA, 1991.

Prayers for the Domestic Church: A Handbook for Worship in the Home (revised ed.). Edward Hays, Forest Peace, Easton, KS, 1989.

THE CHALLENGE OF SHARING YOUR FAITH

1. The Element of Change

Childhood begins when a youngster asks where he came from and ends when he refuses to tell you where he is going.

Dorothea Kent
The Joy of Family

The changes taking place in children between the ages of seven and fourteen shake up family relationships. These changes can cause deeper commitment and growth — or lead to disintegration. Understanding the changes children go through during these years will enrich our family's life as a community and help us share faith in the home. Although these years can be tumultuous and trying, they can also be exciting and fun when viewed with the proper perspective.

Children do not move through the developmental stages of growth in isolation. They grow up within a family system. Just as the growth of flowers depends upon the amount of care and attention they receive, so too with children. They respond to the family system that surrounds them.

The opposite of this statement is also true. A family's growth, happiness, and sense of well-being are strongly influenced by the stages children pass through on their way to maturity. The family is "not a collection of individuals, but a living developing system whose parts are essentially interconnected" *(A Family Perspective in Church and Society)*.

Picture your family as a mobile. When it's resting in perfect balance, it is most comfortable. As long as each member plays the role expected by others and no winds of change blow, everything stays calm. But when one person changes — by wanting more independence, by becoming sick, by transferring jobs — the whole family mobile shifts and bounces around. This disturbs everyone in some way. Yet, the movement allows growth and change to take place. You can look at change as a disturbing inconvenience or as a sign of life. The only things and people who don't change are dead things and people.

This book is designed to help you create the rich environment of mutual respect and understanding that will ensure your family's growth in all ways, especially in ways of faith.

Belonging and Separating

Children in the early and middle childhood years need a sense of belonging to a family, especially as they enter new and sometimes threatening social groups outside the home. As they begin to measure themselves against others, their self-esteem might be threatened. They need the security of knowing their family is there for them, no matter what. They need a strong sense of belonging.

At the same time, however, these children's energies are directed toward establishing who they are as individuals separate from their family. Often they will test new roles and identities that are contrary to their parents' expectations. So, while they need the security of knowing their family is there for them, they also need to experience themselves as individuals separate from the family unit.

Because the family is an interdependent system, every member of the family will experience tension when the grade-school child urgently asks, "How can I be a separate person and still belong to this family?"

This tension is a normal part of the emancipation process and a necessary and stage-appropriate task for full maturity. Understanding this can help your family system function more smoothly through these stages of development.

Your Family of Origin

The way you respond to changes in your children's development will be shaped by the way your own parents responded to you during your childhood and adolescent years. You'll probably tend to do one of two things: you'll parent in the same style your parents did or you'll react to their parenting style by doing just the opposite of what they did. Parents pass on attitudes about what makes a girl "feminine" or a boy "masculine." Parents' attitudes toward sex, money, popularity, success, and acceptance affect their children's attitudes toward these same issues.

Children become increasingly aware of the differences between families: their own and others. In grade-school and early adolescent years, children challenge their parents' authority, their patterns of thought, and their behavior. "That's the way we've always done it" is not a satisfactory answer for children who are beginning to think logically.

You may discover that you're doing and saying things just like your own parents did, despite your good intentions to "never do that to my kids." It's not uncommon for you to hear yourself admonishing your children and to suddenly realize, as one mother put it (and not too happily), "I've just turned into my own mother!"

There are, of course, many healthy values and behaviors from your family of origin that you can and do pass on to your children. It is wise, however, to be alert for the destructive or unhealthy habits and attitudes that might surface; avoid passing those on to your own children.

In their book *Growing Up Again: How to Parent Yourself So You Can Parent Your Children,* Jean Clarke and Connie Dawson insist that "we need to repair what didn't get done in our own childhood in order to parent better." Parents who grew up in homes where alcohol, drugs, chronic illness, extreme poverty, unexpected tragedies, or addictive and compulsive behaviors were present may have been reared in a shame-filled or neglectful home situation. This would have made it difficult, if not impossible, for these parents to grow emotionally and spiritually in their own grade-school years.

The changes in your grade-school-age child will challenge your family system to examine itself. In fact, it can stimulate healthy growth. If you want to parent in patterns different from the way you were parented or if you want to change your pattern of parenting, consider reading some of the material suggested in the resource listing on page 56. In some cases, you and your family may find counseling helpful in resolving serious long-term conflicts or harmful behavior patterns that pass from generation to generation.

If your family of origin had a strong ethnic or cultural identity, your children's entrance into the larger world outside the family may be particularly challenging. Up until about age seven, you may have been able to imitate the unique ethnic or cultural values of your own parents. But a Hispanic father who grew up in Mexico surrounded by grandparents and *los padrinos* (the godparents) will be unable to duplicate for his own child his childhood experience in this society of highly mobile, privatized nuclear families. A young mother raised in a small midwestern farming community will have to make adjustments in expectations for her own child's school experiences in the Los Angeles metropolitan area.

As your children establish their own unique personalities and skills in grade-school years, reflect on your family-of-origin experience. Sort out what is unnecessary or impossible to pass on and consciously transmit what is healthy and life-giving. This process helps create strong family systems — and strong faith emerges from strong families.

Parenting Alone

Single parents have special challenges during the grade-school years. Some days there are simply more places to go and things to do than one parent can possibly handle. The pace of life, the complexity of disciplining children alone, and the tug of children wanting to belong and yet separate from the family unit can lead to physical and emotional exhaustion.

Surviving and thriving single parents encourage one another to accept offers of help from other parents, particularly with chauffeuring and childcare. "Don't be too proud," says one single-parent mother of five children. "God cares for us by working through other people. I do the very best I can, but I feel free to accept, and I am very grateful for any help I can get."

Many single parents find a support group to be helpful on days when frustration runs high. "It's been my survival," explains one parent, "just to be able to call someone anytime and talk things over."

Though sharing hopes and cares is an important part of the special intimacy persons share within the family, there are some emotional issues that are not appropriate burdens for children. A child may try to be the "man" or the "woman" of the house and play an adult role with other children. Doing this does not allow for the normal developmental stages of childhood. Having a friend or support group helps single parents cope — and grow — and allows children their rightful experience of being children.

If you are a single parent, take time and space for yourself each day. This is not being selfish; it's essential. Renew your energy. The time you put aside, even though it seems impossible, may make the difference between surviving and thriving as a single parent.

Since your child changes so often in the grade-school years, be alert for signs of renewed grief or loss that may resurface long after the loss of the parent. An eight-year-old deals with loss on one level; at thirteen, that same child will have new issues to face with regard to that same loss. Allow your child to work out his or her feelings along the way; your strength as a single-parent family will deepen.

Parenting as a Couple

All through their parenting years, couples need to take time for themselves. Otherwise, parents can unconsciously let tensions and hectic schedules weaken their marriage. The most important thing parents can do for a healthy family is to love each other, show that love, and take time to nurture their own loving relationship.

As children grow, their lives — and therefore your lives — become increasingly busy. Count on it. If you have only one child, the number of activities on your family calendar will double when that child enters the grade-school years. If you have more than one child, the number of activities rises exponentially. Accommodating your children's needs during this time will eat away at the time you have together.

If you're in a two-career family, the burden of arranging childcare and adjusting work schedules to meet family commitments will place additional strains on your relationship. At the end of the day, you find yourselves thirsty for understanding, comfort, companionship, quiet, and intimacy — but with empty pitches. Much marital conversation deals with children's needs and activities. Add illness and other anxious circumstances to the family, and the tension increases. If you have a child who has a disability, your relationship takes on another layer of stress.

Your child's movement into early adolescence will test your patience and authority. A divided couple is an advantage to a child; playing one parent against the other is an old trick. Recognizing this, you can stand together on important issues. Of course, you won't always agree. But honest disagreement worked out in healthy discussions is good for children to hear. Undermining each other's authority is destructive.

The very best way to assure a united front between the two of you when it comes to your children is to keep the lines of communication open and nurture your own loving relationship. How do you do this?

Some couples plan dates each week, rise early on a Saturday morning for breakfast, or have late night dinners after the children are in bed. If relatives can provide childcare, a weekend away can help build a marriage relationship eroded by a frantic schedule. If relatives are not available, friends might take turns giving one another a day or weekend away.

Prayer is another strengthening factor. Marital-satisfaction studies show that couples who pray together stay together. If you feel awkward beginning a tradition of prayer with your spouse, try it for a week or during Lent or Advent. Begin with simple memorized prayers, a short passage from Scripture, or a simple spontaneous prayer of gratitude. The material mentioned in the following resource listing suggests several books that would be helpful in starting this tradition.

Resources

Family Matters: A Layman's Guide to Family Functioning. Thomas A. Power, Elan Publishing Co., Santa Barbara, CA, 1989.

Generation to Generation: Family Process in Church and Synagogue. Edwin H. Friedman, Guilford Press, New York, 1985.

Growing Up Again: How to Parent Yourself So You Can Parent Your Children. Jean I. Clarke and Connie Dawson, Harper San Francisco, San Francisco, 1989.

Marrying Well: Stages on the Journey of Christian Marriage. Evelyn E. Whitehead and James D. Whitehead, Doubleday, New York, 1983.

2. Ordinary Ways of Sharing Your Faith

A child needs encouragement like a plant needs water.
Rudolph Dreikurs

We share faith in conscious and unconscious ways. Formal religious ceremonies are a rich part of Catholic tradition. Building children's faith, however, is also dependent upon the ordinary occurrences that take place in a loving family environment. This is where we build confidence, promote individuality, and give children a sense of belonging. As loving parents, we are already doing many of these things.

This chapter includes suggestions for ordinary faith-building activities.

A Sense of Acceptance

At the heart of the Catholic Christian tradition is the belief that God loves us without condition. We hold a rich tradition of Yahweh's covenant, completed in Christ's unconditional gift of himself to us in the New Testament. Believing in covenant love is central to being a faith-filled person. Children need to know they are accepted and loved in just this same unconditional way.

Yet, we all know those days when we don't even remotely *like* our children. To understand how we can love our children, and still not like them, it helps to visualize our children in grave danger. The immediate surge of protective love shows us how we can dislike what they are saying and doing and still love them. The fact that children need our love most when they are least lovable constitutes our greatest parental challenge.

The following parenting techniques help us show our children acceptance, encouragement, and unconditional love.

Express your affection. In gentle ways, convey love and appreciation to your children. Every day, let some action say to them "I love you."

Display that you can accept them while not accepting their actions. While recognizing the unacceptable behavior in your children and providing consistent and realistic consequences, affirm your children's basic goodness.

Be extravagant in your expressions at times. After all, God loves us with an extravagance beyond our imaginations. As mere mortals, we can't possibly love that way — but we can aspire toward it.

Let your children know that you have positive expectations for them. Give them a deep-seated sense of personal potential. Let them know that you believe in them, that you respect their capabilities, and that you value them as individuals. If you believe it, they will too.

A Sense of Belonging

Whenever you let your children know that you are happy they're in your life and that they have a special place in the family and community, you lay the foundation for faith in a personal loving God and in the community of people gathered as one Body of Christ.

Catholics and other Christians see themselves as God's people. God said, "I will be your God, and you will be my people" (Leviticus 26:12). This covenant refers to both a personal and a community relationship. We "belong" to one another. The gospel call to care for one another as Christians comes from that belonging to one another. We are brothers and sisters of Christ and children of the same Mother-Father God.

This tenet of faith can seem abstract and meaningless to children between the ages of seven and fourteen, when separation is a part of the task at hand. Only if children have some lived experience of belonging can this dimension of faith be realized.

Here are some examples of how we can create that sense of belonging.

Preserve your child's history. Create and share family picture albums and home movies showing your children's history. When divorce or death separates children from part of their family or when children enter into a new family in a second marriage, their sense of belonging is preserved in these links to the past. Allow your children to grieve lost relationships while building on a strong foundation for belonging to the new family system.

Share family stories. Share memories about family members who have died or who live far away. Remember sad and happy, somber and playful, silly and wise things about these people.

Establish and/or carry on family traditions. Use food, games, and other activities to mark your traditions. Cherish objects with sentimental value. Build on holiday traditions or celebrations that are unique to your own family. In a world of constantly changing circumstances, children need roots that connect them with someone or something safe and secure. Experts and families themselves have recognized the important role that rituals and traditions play in expressing faith and in bringing families together.

Be there for your child; be dependable and trustworthy. Be in a supportive role at recitals, games, and school programs. Be fully present to your children when they're scared, sick, depressed, confused, and joyful. Keep your word; do not make extravagant promises or empty threats.

These and other daily signs of our faithfulness and commitment to the family we live with are important in helping children understand a God who has said to us, "I will not leave you orphans; I will come to you" (John 14:18).

A Sense of Self-worth

Parenting our children in healthy ways that build self-worth and encourage respect for the dignity of all human and natural life is a critical element in the formation of faith. Unless we truly regard ourselves as lovable and good, we cannot believe that we are Christ-bearers or that God could find a home in our hearts. Healthy self-love and the self-esteem that follows from it are necessary before we can treat others with respect, seek justice in relationships, and peacefully resolve conflicts.

Catholics are incarnational people. We believe that Jesus became one of us, with all the fears and pains, strengths and limitations, that are part of the essence of human nature. We believe that by our baptism we share in God's life in us, that each of us, frail and imperfect, is created in God's image. At Christmas, we celebrate Emmanuel, God-With-Us.

Here are some suggestions for building the self-worth that gives our children the courage to be Christ-bearers.

Use positive discipline measures in parenting. Be sure your children know what's expected of them, and that consequences for improper behavior will be appropriate and consistent. Avoid blaming, threatening, verbal put-downs, and harsh punishment. Make sure your childcare provider uses the same philosophy. Excellent classes and books are available to help develop constructive and positive parenting techniques.

Give your child age-appropriate responsibilities. Help your children build confidence in their abilities to complete tasks and reap the self-esteem that flows from that. In the grade-school years, children display rapidly improving physical, intellectual, and social skills. Entrust children with tasks appropriate to their age and personal development, affirming them as they take on new and more challenging responsibilities.

Affirm your child's individuality. Praise your children's special qualities — kindness, generosity, honesty, humor — as well as what they achieve. Each of us is created uniquely gifted. Especially in early adolescence, children need your assurance that they are, indeed, gifted and unique. They need to hear from you that it's okay for them to be just who they are.

Concentrate on improvement, not perfection. Give strokes for small steps. Work with positive expectations and treat mistakes as educational tools.

A Sense of Compassion

We must have some human experience of forgiveness if we are to believe in a forgiving God. Without that experience, it's difficult, if not impossible, for children to believe that God forgives them. A loving family environment certainly provides ample opportunities for forgiveness.

Somewhere around the age of eight, our children will be invited by the Church to prepare for the sacrament of reconciliation. This sacrament ritualizes an important tenet of the Catholic faith: we are loved by God without condition, thus forgiveness and grace are always available to us. We are not forgiven simply because we are sorry or because of the priest's power to absolve. We are forgiven because of who God is and particularly because of the life and actions of Jesus Christ.

Grade-school children develop the ability to process abstract ideas and values. Somewhere between eight and eleven, they begin to understand rules for order in their relationships. Their ability to make choices based on these rules and values will improve. When they fail to choose wisely, they need to know that they are forgiven and can try again. Providing experiences of forgiveness at home and at church can strengthen their faith in themselves and in a compassionate, loving God.

Here are some ordinary ways to do this.

Make family forgiveness a habit. It is easier to develop a habit of forgiving one another in parent and sibling relationships at age seven than it is at age fourteen. So start early.

Apologize to your child when you've behaved inappropriately. Teaching children the language of reconciliation is important. Encourage them to say "I am sorry I slammed the door in your face" by saying it yourself when you're responsible. Teach them to respond, "I forgive you."

Forgiveness takes two: one asking for forgiveness and the other forgiving. Often when children apologize, our response is simply "Okay, that's all right, no big deal," or we say nothing at all. These responses imply that hurting another is not wrong or that an apology is not important. The response "I forgive you" along with eye contact or a simple physical expression of affection ensures that forgiveness has been extended. This experience prepares children to appreciate God's forgiveness and to forgive others as well.

Model forgiveness. Display a genuine compassion in all your relationships. As children enter early adolescence, they will begin to point out inconsistencies in our behavior. Modeling forgiveness and compassion rather than revenge is the best teacher. When you find it difficult to forgive your coworkers, family members, or friends, admit it. Sometimes holding out the value and importance of forgiveness is all we can do in modeling forgiveness.

A Sense of Community

Nothing creates a family's sense of "one-ness" better than sharing meals together. Breaking bread together — for breakfast, after school, dinner, or nighttime snacks — is a perfect time to share news — especially the Good News — in a loving family community.

Catholic Christians have a distinct and rich tradition of gathering around the Lord's table at Sunday Mass. The Eucharist, taken from the Greek word *thanksgiving,* is the community's experience of Christ's presence that nourishes and strengthens believers for life's journey. Belief in the presence of Christ in the Eucharist is an important part of our children's faith development.

Parishes have well-developed programs to prepare your children for first Communion. This is a good time to decide on a specific parish community for worship, if you have not done so previously. Your children's experience of participation in a more grown-up way at Mass will then be affirmed and recognized by the larger community, including your children's peers. Being prepared for this faith passage with peers in a Christian community helps your children see its value and significance.

There are some ordinary rituals and experiences at home that will make it possible for your children to build a deep and simple understanding of the Eucharist.

Take time to break bread as a family. Families' eating habits have changed substantially in the last fifty years. Often, food is "dispensed" instead of shared. Children frequently prepare their own food and eat alone. Members of the family eat together in front of the television or with a newspaper or magazine between them.

If a family never shares a meal, the eucharistic concept of "banquet" as shared meal is difficult to grasp. It's never too late, however, to start a new tradition. Enjoy the enriching experience of gathering around food with conversation, attention to one another, thanksgiving, and recognition that the food comes from God's bounty and goodness.

You may need to jockey schedules so the family can eat together at least occasionally. Make it a priority. If all members of your family can't be together because of scheduling, share a meal with whomever can be there.

Mealtime should not be used to correct children or allow them to complain about one another. Establish some simple ground rules when children are small; share plans, dreams, and activities, and give thanks. Insist that the tradition be carried on as the family grows. Teenagers will probably complain, but this time together will provide them with good memories.

Tap into the value of ritual meals. There are special events that heighten children's appreciation for a community meal: birthdays, anniversaries, graduations, and weddings. Even a child's passing to a new level at swimming class can be a time to reinforce the value of eating together. Involve your children in planning and preparation as well as saying grace or thanksgiving for these meals. Some families have the tradition of the honored child getting to use a special plate or mug. When children celebrate first Communion at ages eight or nine, their understanding will be simple and concrete. As they mature, they will think more abstractly. Then the rich meaning of the whole eucharistic tradition of sacrificial love and covenant relationship will build upon ordinary daily experiences with others.

Attend Mass regularly. Actions speak louder than words, and most children do not enjoy being dropped off alone at a community celebration. If you've had some negative experiences at Mass or have lost the habit of celebrating Mass regularly, your child's first Communion can be a time to renew that aspect of your own faith life so you can fully share this rich faith tradition.

Attend a class or read some current literature on the Mass. Update and deepen your understanding of the value of the Eucharist. If you are divorced or separated and unsure of your relationship to the sacramental life of the Church, be assured that your Catholic faith family awaits you with open arms. Talk to a trusted member of your church community.

A Sense of Service and Mission

All Christians recognize the gospel message to love and serve others: feed the poor, clothe the naked, protect the orphan, provide for the widow, and so forth. Although many of these tasks have been taken over by social-service agencies, the truth remains that "the poor you will always have with you" (Matthew 26:11).

In the media, and to some extent in the community, our children are confronted with extreme material and spiritual poverty. Giving them the skills and opportunity to serve others, even in some small way on a regular basis, allows them to see the face of Christ in others. It also helps ward off the numbness and complacency that comes with being overwhelmed by so much poverty. They begin to feel that they can make a difference.

There are simple ways to develop a sense of mission. These may already be a part of your everyday life.

Channel your child's energy into helping others. Grade-school children normally have boundless energy. Shoveling a walk for the neighbor or helping with a local food drive are short-term endeavors that develop a healthy habit of helping others. For early adolescents, active participation in the service of others is an effective way to teach children the basics of faithful living when classroom learning and reflection among peers are less appealing to them.

Again, parental modeling of this kind of behavior is the best teaching tool. When your child celebrates confirmation, the teaching Church will assist you in reinforcing the important responsibility mature Christians have toward one another. Your parish youth group can act as support to you in encouraging service to others outside your home.

Let charity begin at home. Use the liturgical seasons of Advent and Lent to consciously plan acts of kindness and service to one another at home and in your extended family. As they get older, brothers and sisters often don't see the value of serving one another. Encourage some personal sacrifice for others at home as well as outside the home. Certain seasons of the year help families focus on their mission as domestic church, loving and serving one another at home. You may have some traditions already established. If not, ask local religious bookstores, your parish staff, or the diocesan family-life office for materials with suggestions for doing this.

Expand your child's view of the world. Families living in a nation that has the lowest percent of the world's population using the greatest percent of the world's resources can easily become blind to the poverty and misery that most of the world's population struggles with. Encourage a deep respect for earth and a sense of stewardship toward all its resources. Develop in your children an appreciation for the rich diversity of race, color, and culture that inhabit their planet.

Children like to get involved in causes and be part of the solution, if they understand the problem. Many helpful materials exist for your family's use, including the practical *Parenting for Peace and Justice Newsletter.*

A Sense of Awe

In the Scriptures, Jesus uses the stuff of ordinary life to show his presence and power. Losing at an athletic event, getting a good grade in school, finding a new friend, being left out of a birthday party, losing a grandparent, or welcoming a baby sister or cousin are all sacred moments of awe in which we can experience God's presence as a family.

Even monotonous daily routines like getting up in the morning, going to work or school, and doing dishes together can be experiences of the sacred. In her book *Sacred Dwelling,* Wendy Wright calls families to reflect on their ordinary lived experiences and see God present there. Several other books mentioned in the resource listing on pages 69-70 might help you get into the habit of seeing God in the ordinary.

You will also find God's awesome presence in some of the following ordinary dimensions of daily life.

The awe of nature: Enjoy and give thanks for nature with your children: orange and pink sunsets, birds chirping at sunrise, the changing of the seasons. The silent appreciation of these natural wonders provides a sense of the sacred for you and for your children.

The experience of new life and death: Both nature and family life provide rich experiences in creation's pattern of new life out of death. With your children, marvel at the tiny fingers and toes of a newborn. At appropriate moments, grieve and cry with your children, honestly recognizing the fragileness of human life. When the eleven adult children, their spouses, and the twenty-nine grandchildren of John Stockwell wrote messages on his simple wooden casket and released balloons to accompany him on his journey, the cathartic release of mutual tears was a sacred celebration. The section on "Loss and Grief" (page 124) will help you share with your children a Christian perspective about death.

The splendor of fun: Laughter, games, and fun can bring families together in circumstances that provide healing, encouragement, and a sense of God's gracious presence in a home. The ability to laugh together, at ourselves and with one another, is an important indication of our mental and physical health. Laughter in itself is like a minivacation or internal jogging. It's good for you and for your family.

The spiritual works of homemaking: Clothing the naked, feeding the hungry, and sheltering the homeless are the ordinary tasks Christ used to separate the saved from those who were not. This includes the necessary duties of a homemaker. Though they may not seem to be specifically religious actions, washing and mending clothes, grocery shopping, making dinner, and working to provide a home for your family are among the works of mercy that Christ used as a measure of our salvation.

A Sense of Gratitude

The central act of worship in the Christian community is Eucharist, which means "thanksgiving." The long history of God's relationship with people, from Abraham to Jesus, tells of a gracious love for and action on behalf of those who believe. Catholic Christians believe that human life is a gift of the creator God, and that Jesus is the gift of God's very self to us. The Eucharist is Jesus' gift of himself to his followers. At every Mass, these gifts are celebrated, and the community is called to thanksgiving and praise.

Christians believe that all good things come from God. Catholic theology and social teaching reflect this truth and challenge society's myth of the self-made person. Children who grow up in a "the-world-owes-me" environment may find it difficult to recognize God's gifts in the people and events around them. This recognition of the generous gift of life and love is at the foundation of Christian moral and ethical principles. Part of getting our children to live by the principles of appreciating God's gifts is moving them toward an "attitude of gratitude" to God in all things.

The following suggestions can help you develop this attitude in your children.

Talk about life's goodness. Point out that which is sweet, comfortable, and good in terms of gift and gratitude. Recognizing flowers, lakes, and the beauties of nature as God's gifts of creation fosters a sense of responsibility for the earth. That sense will be built on gratitude, not legislation. Pointing out your children's talents and abilities as gifts from God encourages self-confidence tempered by humility. To be humble is not to deny one's abilities. It is to recognize where they come from.

Avoid relegating catastrophes and tragic human events to "God's will." God does not — and cannot — cause evil or pain. Telling children that God "wanted our baby in heaven" or that the destruction of a whole village of people was God's will creates a negative image of God, one to whom it is difficult to be grateful. Emphasizing that God weeps with and comforts those who are in pain points toward what our own human response to tragedy should be. The resources suggested in the section titled "Loss and Grief" (page 124) may help you work through these difficult situations without blaming God.

Look for and name the good in events and people around you. Looking for the good in people rather than criticizing their imperfections helps put your own imperfections in perspective. Offer thanks and praise to God each day for what is good. An optimist sees rain for it's value in watering lawns and flowers; a pessimist will grump about the discomfort and humidity. Be an optimist; model an attitude of gratitude.

Be countercultural in a gospel sense. For Catholic Christians, being a person of faith often means living counterculturally. We have a special awareness of the brotherhood and sisterhood of the human family, the dignity of human life, the value of sacrificial love for others, hope in new life out of death, and the passing value of consumer products. Many of the previous suggestions parallel the traits of healthy families. In recent studies, families and experts found that there are some traits that healthy families have in common. One of them is family faith and religious traditions. The following resource listing mentions books that explain the characteristics of healthy families and give advice to parents.

Two-parent, single-parent, and adoptive or blended families can all give their children some healthy fundamental experiences for knowing God and belonging to a faith community of Catholic Christians in the ordinary events and actions of family living.

Resources

Building Shalom Families (VHS tape, guidebook, and five workshops). James McGinnis and Kathleen McGinnis, Institute for Peace and Justice, 4144 Lindell Boulevard, #400, St. Louis, MO 63108, 1986.

Christian Families in the Real World. Mitch Finley and Kathy Finley, Thomas More Press, Chicago, 1984.

Creating a Loving Family: A Practical Handbook for Catholic Parents. Bridget Meehan, SSC, D.Min., Liguori Publications, Liguori, MO, 1992.

Finding God at Home: Family Life as Spiritual Discipline. Ernest Boyer, Harper San Francisco, San Francisco, 1988.

Parenting for Peace and Justice Newsletter. The Institute for Peace and Justice, 4144 Lindell Boulevard, #400, St. Louis, MO 63108.

Sacred Dwelling: A Spirituality of Family Life. Wendy Wright, Crossroad/Continuum Publishing Group, New York, 1990.

Starting Out Right: Nurturing Young Children as Peacemakers. Kathleen McGinnis and Barbara Oehlberg, Meyer Stone Books, New York, 1988.

Traits of a Healthy Family. Dolores Curran, Ballantine, New York, 1984.

3. Faith Generators for Your Children

Our children will have faith if we have faith and are faithful. Both we and our children will have Christian faith if we join with others in a worshiping, learning, witnessing Christian community of faith.

John H. Westerhoff, III
Will Our Children Have Faith?

We teach Christian values by sharing the facts about our faith. More importantly, we teach by how we act upon those values in relationship with others — especially our children. The old saying "Faith is caught not taught" is accurate. If we cherish Christian beliefs and values and try to live them daily, our children will be nurtured by our personal example. A faith-filled home environment is the most important element in our child's spiritual growth.

Our children's faith is also nurtured by people, events, and resources available inside and outside the home. For example, a caring teacher, a retreat experience, a role model like Mother

Teresa, a moving liturgy, or a gentle parish priest can nurture our children's faith development in many ways. Our love and trust in God will enrich these experiences.

Your Unique Example

Parents generate faith in their children in many different ways. Some express faith by being involved in ministry with the homeless. Others go to Medjugorje. Some express their faith through devotion to Mary or particular saints. Some protest the buildup of nuclear arms, teach religion classes, or pray the rosary. Some parents experience God's presence intellectually through an interest in theology and spirituality. Some experience faith through music, poetry, or encounters with others. Some deeply experience their faith in God while fishing, hiking, or —yes — even golfing.

You have to be comfortable and natural with the way you nourish a faith-filled environment for your children. We've just reviewed some ordinary ways that all parents can use to promote a faith-ready environment. Your personal example, on the other hand, like yeast in bread, will be the ingredient that helps make it all happen.

Talk. Mentioning God's presence and power in the ordinary flow of things helps children expand their image of God. Although too much "Jesus this" and "Jesus that" may numb children's sensitivity to the Divine, sincere acknowledgment of God in your everyday life will make God's loving presence a reality. Children who hear the name of Jesus only in the atmosphere of anger or tension will have a limited image of God.

You can speak of God by acknowledging the work of the Holy Spirit in everyday conversation. Comment on God's goodness in the beauty of a fresh snowfall. Point out the importance of being stewards of the earth when recycling cans. Express gratitude to God after a good night's rest. What we're looking for is the kind of realization that was expressed by a six-year-old standing in awe before the majestic view of Lewis and Clark Lake: "I just feel God all around me."

Worship. Your attendance at Mass on Sunday — or more frequently during Lent and Advent — tells your children that worshiping God is an important activity. Show your appreciation for the communal aspects of Mass: take your family toward the front where your children with shorter earth suits can see. Acknowledge the efforts of the liturgy committee in a kindly fashion. Point out the changing liturgical symbols. Let your children become familiar with both the surroundings and the actions of worship. It shapes their understanding and appreciation of Eucharist and community.

Pray. Let your children see and hear you praying at home, at church, and elsewhere. Children who see their parent(s) pray nightly before bed will carry that image with them forever.

Listen. Listen intently to your children's questions about God and the meaning of life's events. When your children are upset, listen to what they say and then without judgment or criticism repeat back to them what you've heard them say. "It sounds as if you have a problem with this" or "Tell me more about how you feel" opens the lines of communication.

If your child says, "I hate going to religion class," an active listening response would be "It sounds as if you're really upset about going to class right now." This conveys acceptance, love, and respect and helps turn the discussion in a constructive direction. Continued active listening and repeating the child's thoughts help the child develop insight and work toward a solution. There are a number of books available that will guide you in this important technique for nurturing your child.

When children question you on matters of faith, give answers appropriate to their level of understanding. When you don't know the answer, or the answer is shrouded in mystery, admit that. This encourages children to continue their faith search.

At seven, your child's questions about God and human events

will stem from a need for reassurance rather than a desire for understanding theological concepts. Listen carefully to your child's questions; ask questions yourself that might help the child get in touch with specific fears and concerns. Offer the child an assurance of your love, no matter what.

As children move toward adolescence, their questions become more probing. They grow out of the notion that their parents are perfect and begin to see that even a loving God does not prevent pain and suffering. Their bewilderment and doubt may begin to worry you — yet, this is a natural part of the maturing process. Questions and doubts move children from one level of faith to a deeper level. As your children explore difficult questions, join in the process of reflecting on the mysteries of life — thus displaying to your children that seeking truth and understanding is a lifelong process.

No parent, or theologian for that matter, can present a vision of life that is absolutely certain or without doubt. Mature Christian faith trusts in God's goodness and faithfulness, not in surefire answers.

Protect. To some extent, you have to shield your children's faith from influences in society that may threaten it. More than any other time in modern history, children are exposed to influences that will contradict Christian principles: respect for human life and the commandment to love.

Grade-school children are naturally curious. As they mature, they become more daring. They may be exposed to Ouija™ boards, cults, satanic influences, pornography, and violence of every kind. Although it is impossible to eliminate these influences altogether, you can set limits on what media and written materials you allow into your home.

Firm guidelines concerning television and the media are necessary during grade-school years. Children should understand these guidelines and be aware of your expectations. If these guidelines are not met, consequences should be appropriate and certain.

Your parental control will lessen significantly as your children begin to spend less time at home. Even if your children see and hear these influences at friends' homes, it is important that they know what the values and limits are in their own home.

The Role of Others

The Catholic Christian tradition emphasizes the importance of community; no one goes to God alone. Each child is baptized into a faith community that includes family, friends, neighbors, parish, the larger Church, and the world. The Holy Spirit works through all these in generating the faith of each individual.

Many persons share the gift of faith with our children — and this is a comforting thought. Our primary role is to help other persons, events, and resources become positive influences in fanning the flame of faith in our children.

Our children witness many occasions of faith in action: the fervent nighttime prayers of a younger sister, the example of an older brother who volunteers to tutor a child with a learning disability, or the friend who serves Mass during the summer months. It is unlikely, however, that our children will acknowledge the influence of these occasions until they are adults and reflect on how they became who they are becoming.

Aunts and uncles: If your child has an aunt or uncle who attends daily Mass or has a particular devotion that expresses faith in God, invite that person to spend time with your child. Encourage a rapport that holds the potential for impacting your child's faith in powerful ways. Don't, however, force any relationship on your children.

Grandparents: Grandma and Grandpa often have more time and energy to read stories and listen patiently to questions and concerns. When Grandma and Grandpa share stories from their past, your children get a sense of their own history and roots. With this vision, your children are better prepared to search for an identity that is characteristic of their particular stage of faith development.

If grandparents live far away or are gone, encourage your children to adopt a neighbor or local nursing-home resident who is a person of faith. Children live intensely in the present moment; providing them with older friends broadens their perspective about the immediacy of things. In informal surveys, adults were asked who were key faith examples and influences in childhood. Grandparents usually are on the top of the list.

Godparents: Don't overlook these people who played a key role in the initiation of your children into the Church. Invite them to remain active in your children's lives. Once again, cultivate a friendship that is rooted in a common faith tradition. Ask them to accompany you and your children to Mass on a regular basis. Encourage them to celebrate the key sacramental moments in your children's lives.

Other adult mentors: Teachers, youth ministers, Scout leaders, 4-H leaders, pastoral ministers, priests, nuns, and faith-filled neighbors and friends can assist you in generating faith in your children. Part of your task is to facilitate the relationships and experiences that will enhance faith whenever possible.

Teachable Moments

Teachable moments are those times when God's presence and power can be felt in ways that deepen the faith of all those present. At the tragic death of their eighteen-year-old son and brother, a family struggled with the role God has in such sad events. At the same time, the family experienced the overwhelming love of God at the funeral and during their days of grieving. This came to them through the boy's friends, neighbors, and the members of their parish community. Thousands of cards, offers of help, visits from friends, and gifts of food testified to the faithful care God had for that family in their time of trial.

Teachable moments abound. They are spectacular — and subtle; they are extraordinary — and ordinary.

Teachable moments in the ordinary: Some teachable moments are so ordinary that they almost pass unnoticed. Moving up an inch on the growth chart, scoring a point in a soccer game, and finding blossoms on the growing tomato plant are ordinary moments of celebration and wonder at the gift of life and growth. A full-colored rainbow, a beautiful sunrise, a star-scattered night sky, fresh bed-sheets flapping in the breeze, can all be teachable moments. A simple, heartfelt "Thank you, Lord" says it all at times like this. When children develop respect and gratitude for the life of the earth, their concerns and questions about contemporary problems of war and pollution will come from a deep reverence for life rather than from fear.

While your children are young, you are privileged to share experiences of the sacred that transcend theology or formal teaching about God.

Teachable moments in media events: News coverage of the fall of the Berlin Wall and papal visits, documentaries on the work of missionaries in South America, and human-interest stories about the conditions of the homeless provide your children with an expanded view of faith-filled people and events in the larger human family. Interviews with astronauts after interplanetary travel and victims spared destruction by earthquakes show children that faith in God is something that goes beyond family and school.

Explaining and discussing what's wrong with an offensive ad or why a certain program cannot be watched are also teachable moments.

Teachable moments in magnificent celebrations: Several years ago a celebration called "Loved and Sent" brought together twelve thousand parents and children. They gathered at an enormous field house for a liturgical celebration of evangelization in the Archdiocese of Omaha. The sheer magnitude of the event — it's assembled choirs and musicians, banners and balloons, ethnic costumes and brightly vested processions — contributed to a spectacular experience of praise and worship.

Public celebrations of this magnitude, or even on a smaller scale, teach children about faith. Such events do not need your added comments. When you seize these opportunities, you'll learn — years later — that these moments made lasting impressions on your children.

The larger Church community can provide a variety of teachable moments for your children. Local retreat programs or special peer-group weekends may be available through your diocesan offices. Family retreats are particularly formative moments for families of grade-school children. The resource listing below offers information on some of these events.

Many programs are available for families experiencing difficulties such as divorce or the death of a parent. Schools and parishes offer peer-support programs that help children remove the obstacles to faith growth that may develop after loss.

Serving as an altar server and singing in the choir are opportunities for children to participate directly in the liturgical life of their parishes. These experiences can provide the important peer-association needed as children mature. Mission field trips, service projects, and cultural-awareness activities challenge your children to take action on what they believe.

Tap into those opportunities outside your home that can be faith generators for your children. This does not lessen your parental responsibility and privilege. Rather, extending this privilege to others makes the awesome responsibility sit easier on your shoulders.

Resources

Bringing Religion Home. The newsletter that helps teach religion in the home. Published by Claretian Publications, 205 West Monroe Street, Chicago, IL 60606.

Family Gathering. Stories, prayers, and activities for Catholic Families. Published five times yearly by Hi-Time Publishing Corporation, 12040F West Feerick Street, Wauwatosa, WI 53222.

Family Piece, Family and Faith, The. Published four times yearly by the National Association of Parish Coordinators/ Directors of Religious Education and the National Catholic Educational Association, Wayne F. Smith, editor, National Catholic Education Association, 1077 30th Street, NW, Washington, DC 20007-3852.

Let's Pray Together. A resource for facilitating prayer in the home. A publication of Families for Prayer, 775 Madison Avenue, Albany, NY 12208.

4. Faith Generators for You

Lord, you have made us for yourself,
and our hearts are restless
until they find their rest in you.
Saint Augustine

We sometimes overlook the presence of God in our very midst. In his *Apostolic Exhortation on the Family,* Pope John Paul II calls the home "the domestic church." Christ lives in the Catholic Church through the sacraments, Scriptures, traditions, and in the faithful. Christ is present, also, in the ordinary lives of families: in the busy schedule, the tight budget, the routine arguments, the family vacation, the mundane routine.

Recognizing Christ's presence in our daily lives — as we prepare a meal, fix a bicycle, read a story, finish the family laundry, or simply give our child a loving hug — gives us an appreciation of the most important ways in which we share our faith.

Homemade Holiness

Edward Hays, Catholic priest and author, calls the faith life of the family "homemade holiness." Reflecting on the everyday ways that God is at work within and around us is the first step toward becoming faith generators for our children.

Each family has its own unique spirituality, not marked by incense and bells or organ music, but a spirituality that is manifested in cooking meals, shopping for clothes, playing games, and making house payments. When Jesus separated all those who would be with him in eternity from those who would not (Matthew 25:31-45), one of the measures he used for faithfulness was feeding the hungry, clothing the naked, and sheltering the homeless.

You do these things every day. You may not recognize making a house payment or paying the rent as "sheltering the homeless," but most American families would be homeless if someone wasn't working to make those payments.

Your spiritual life is enfleshed with all-night stints at lowering fevers, spreading lotion on burns, and packing ice on sprains. Your spirituality is sexual with embraces and intimate moments that reconcile differences and reinforce covenant love. Your spiritual life is sacrificial with putting personal desires aside for the good of your children and the family as a whole.

Many of us feel that we can't possibly generate enough energy at the end of the day to pass a bowl of popcorn, let alone pass on faith. We find ourselves low on energy and unable to practice faith as we did before we had a family or even when the family was small. We simply cannot find the time or energy to attend daily Mass or read Scripture or say the rosary on some regular basis. We no longer volunteer at the soup kitchen or take active part in church activities.

Yet, when we show love for our children, when we forgive or are forgiven, we share faith.

Many of us sincerely feel that the most responsible thing to do is leave the spiritual development of our children to others who know more, appear holier, or seem more religious. After all, we don't even have time for our own faith development; where are we going to get energy and time to share faith with our children?

The deep relational life of mothers, fathers, siblings, and extended family members, however, is the fertile soil into which the seeds of faith are planted. The Second Vatican Council emphasized the nature of Church as God's people, the community of believers. In this first and basic community, families and individuals get their first opportunity to break bread together, to forgive and be forgiven, to wash one another's feet (and hands and face!), and love one another as Christ did.

Understanding how all these things work together in our homes — the domestic church — is to realize that sharing the faith is just what we do every day — and in doing that, our own faith is deepened. It takes little physical exertion or time to reflect on this "homemade holiness." A simple prayer in the morning, offering our day to the glory of God, puts the whole day in proper perspective. It also reminds us that the Holy Spirit walks with us.

Prayer

Prayer — both personal prayer and praying as a couple — is an unending source of faith energy. Starting the habit is the hardest part. There is so little time, no quiet space, and very limited amounts of emotional energy to invest in a spiritual exercise such as prayer.

The power of prayer is such, however, that no matter where, when, how much or how little time we spend, we benefit. Books and pamphlets are available to help. Some are mentioned in the resource listing on pages 87-88.

A simple "Thank you, Lord" or "Help, dear Jesus" is a good place to start. Many parents pray for each of their children by name every day. We can add memorized prayers or read the day's

Scriptures. The resource listing also suggests resources for personal and couple prayer. Some parents pray using music with lyrics from Scripture or simple, quiet music for meditation. Others use prayer books with daily prayers or spiritual readings.

Some of us are comfortable praying spontaneously or using centering prayer: choosing a quiet time to let go of our concerns and experience the presence of God. The method or content of our prayer is not as important as developing the habit of daily personal prayer.

Parents who make an effort at private prayer are more likely to gather with children for family prayer. Single parents who want another adult to pray with may wish to find a single-parent prayer partner or a friend to pray for and with. Some personalities prefer solitary prayer, whether married or single. Pastors and pastoral staff are willing to help. Religious bookstores carry a great deal of material on prayer. Do what is comfortable at first and challenge yourself to grow.

Your Formal Religious Education

For some of us, formal religious education ended in our adolescence. Although we may have had some experiences that shaped and deepened our faith since that time, there may have been few opportunities for seriously reflecting on our faith growth or the religious beliefs we accepted as children.

Some of us have had experiences that diminished our faith; we're striving to nourish the spark of faith that smolders within.

Our children's grade-school years provide an environment for us to rekindle or fan the flame of our own faith. As our children learn what it means to be a Christian, a follower of Christ, they will challenge us. Our response to their challenges will demand maturity simply because we have glimpsed the complexity and fragility of human life.

Responding to the question, "What does it mean to be a follower of Christ?" Bernard Cooke, author and theologian, suggests that children and adults need to grasp five fundamentals in order to be a person of faith. Religious understanding is the goal of religious formation. "In such understanding, one does not simply know *about* God as revealed in Jesus the Christ, one *knows* this God."

This does not mean that we must know how to give a complete explanation of the Incarnation to our children. We should be able to recognize and point out those moments when we've encountered the Incarnate Jesus in the healing hands and compassionate hearts of others.

In his article "Basic Christian Understanding" (*Education for Citizenship and Discipleship,* Pilgrim Press, 1989), Cooke proposes a theological framework for faith structured on five fundamentals: the Church, Jesus the Christ, the God who saves, divine/human communication, and authentic Christian life. Our experience of personal faith depends upon some understanding of one or more of these fundamentals. No one grasps them all equally. At one point in life, we may gain new insights into the Church and the presence of Christ alive in the believing community. At another time, we may gain a better understanding of the person of Jesus of Nazareth, the one we "set our hearts on."

Many programs, retreat experiences, books, and tapes are available to help us grow in our religious understanding. Some experiences, such as Cursillo, focus on living an authentic Christian life. They enrich our understanding of what it means, practically, to be a Christian in today's world. Religious understanding goes deeper than acquiring certain knowledge; it also involves how that knowledge affects the way we live.

There are also a large number of parish group activities such as Rite of Christian Initiation for Adults (RCIA), RENEW, and Scripture groups and classes in which you learn about *and* experience faith.

Many parents find Marriage Encounter, Retrouvaille weekends, or involvement in the Christian Family Movement group or Christian Life Community helpful in generating faith. Some parishes offer single-parent networks. Involvement in AA, Al-Anon, grief-support networks, or a Tough Love group helps many parents face crises or transitions with positive growth in faith.

There are groups that help interfaith couples deal with situations that arise from having two faith traditions in a home. These families help one another find practical ways of approaching prayer at home, church attendance, holiday observances, and in-law tensions. These groups help couples find the common denominators from both faith traditions that make for a rich ecumenical family faith.

Ask your parish or diocesan family-life office for information about these groups. If none exist, the resource listing on pages 87-88 will help you get one started or connect you with one elsewhere.

You may view serious family trouble as a kind of "failure" in your faith life. Yet, times of crisis or transition — such as a child's chemical dependency, loss of a job, divorce, or the uprooting of a family — can be what the Japanese call *kiki:* "dangerous opportunities." Families who have experienced serious breakdowns have often found that the crisis brought them closer together and allowed them to heal and grow in faith. With that healing, they became stronger in broken places.

Belonging to a Larger Faith Community

Though the home is the first church and you are the primary religious educators, no home is an island. The trust, love, and forgiveness of the family's spirituality are nourished and guided by participation in the larger Church. In the early centuries of the Church, households of faith formed communities. They cared for one another and preserved their beliefs in the risen Lord. They were countercultural. Catholic parents may find themselves in a similar situation, needing to ban together with other Christians to preserve the faith.

Our society often contradicts Christian beliefs and behaviors. Media and the advertising industry are heralds for a consumer-oriented, competitive, highly individualistic society. Christian values — sacrificial love for others, the dignity of all human life, the sacredness of sex, and the importance of balancing communal and individual needs — are challenged by society. In a violent eye-for-an-eye, competitive world, it is difficult to raise children to be nonviolent, forgiving, and to care for the poor as Christ taught us. Because of this, we need the support of other Christian families in a parish community.

Unfortunately, a personality conflict with a priest or a member of the parish team will cause a person to give up the practice of faith. But priests come and go, as do other ministers in our parish. We can't allow the way we feel about one person to get in the way of practicing our faith in God. A temporary difference of opinion or personality conflict is never so important that it should turn us away from the practice of our faith.

The parish community is a group of families together on the same faith journey. They encourage one another along the way. Believe it or not, we need as much peer acceptance and support as our children. It helps to know other parents who limit their children's TV and movie intake, who spend time together serving others, and who make the sacrifice to celebrate Mass each weekend amidst hectic work and sports schedules.

Though parishes are no longer the center of social life as they used to be fifty years ago, they still provide a gathering place for people who have "set their hearts" on Christ. The parish continues to provide a rich sacramental life, an umbilical cord, through which parents can be nourished with others in faith. It provides the setting for the key family rites of passage surrounding birth, marriage, and death that are celebrated within these believing communities.

The role of adult members of the parish has moved from "pray, pay, and obey" to "celebrate, participate, and collaborate." We make the commitment to live counterculturally, to believe in a world of unbelievers. Participation in such a community strengthens and deepens our faith and enriches family life.

In his *Apostolic Exhortation on the Family (Familiaris Consortio)*, Pope John Paul II emphasizes the importance of "a mutual exchange of presence and help among all the families, each one putting at the service of the others its own experience of life, as well as the gifts of faith and grace." He continues with "...this assistance from family to family will constitute one of the simplest, most effective and most accessible means for transmitting from one to another Christian values" (#69).

In *A Family Perspective in Church and Society,* the United States Conference of Catholic Bishops challenges all institutions, including parishes, to build stronger partnerships with families, to listen to their needs, and to facilitate this exchange of experience and talents between families.

Many parishes offer parenting classes and marriage-enrichment opportunities as a regular part of parish life. These opportunities are offered to enrich good marriages and help good parents be even better. They recognize the important connections between strong marriages, healthy families, and deep faith.

Parishes are like families: there are no perfect ones. If your parish does not offer the kind of support you need as you raise your children in the Catholic tradition, make your needs known to parish leadership. Gather several families with similar concerns and begin to address family-faith issues together. Parish staff or the diocesan family-life office may have resources and training available for family ministry.

You the Teacher; You the Student

Recognizing the face of God at home, practicing daily prayer, taking advantage of continuing-education opportunities, and belonging to a strong faith community generate faith as we fulfill our parenting role. We are, in the real sense, "co-pastors" of the domestic church. There are many other faith generators available to us inside and outside church: in neighborhoods, towns, nationally and globally. One obvious and effective catalyst for personal growth is our own children, those images of God entrusted to our care.

The parenting vocation, based on the covenantal love of Christian faith, allows us to create human life out of love, to form and shape another human being, to be co-creators with God, from the conception of our children to their young adult life. This is an awesome task, one that puts us in intimate relationship with the creator God.

We cannot miss the sacred connection children have with all of life. We see it as we watch them grow and mature through the grade-school years. Our children are profoundly unique in their image and likeness of God.

As children move from seven years of age to fourteen, this sacred connection becomes increasingly clearer. In early childhood, our children's simplicity and curiosity inspired us to enlighten our own image of God. Gathering fall leaves with a child can put you in touch with a powerful sense of the wonder and awe of creation.

In later childhood, children's love of ritual and their insatiable appetite for learning usher us into a new dimension of our own adult faith. Accompanying children on this part of the journey permits us to rediscover the excitement of old traditions and to deepen an understanding of truths left unquestioned since childhood.

One father, helping his teenage daughter learn the gifts of the Holy Spirit, saw the gifts of temperance and fortitude in an entirely new light. The loss of his job and the diagnosis of his wife's multiple sclerosis gave him a fresh appreciation for the gift of fortitude — an appreciation simply not available to him at the inexperienced age of fourteen.

As our children finish grade school, they begin to challenge and scrutinize religious truths and traditions. Their search for what is really "true" and their dissatisfaction with childhood answers to questions about life and death, authority and sex, right and wrong, may disturb us. This disturbance or period of disequilibrium, however, is typical in the transition from one level of faith to the next. It gives us a chance to seek deeper, more mature answers for ourselves; we can go back to where we may have left off at age fourteen.

Stay in touch with the teaching Church during this period of parenting. There is ample material that can assist you — and your child — during this part of your faith journey. This may be a scary period of doubt and turmoil — but you need not venture it alone.

When they look back, many experienced parents conclude that participation in their children's faith journeys was actually a part of their own faith development. This is a journey where Christ is experienced in the breaking of the bread of ordinary lives, where he walks with us as he did with the disciples on the way to Emmaus. Not recognized, but always there, hearing our questioning amid disappointment, sharing our joys and sorrows, reminding us of his promises, and refreshing us with rest stops along the way, Christ is present.

Resources

Dreams Alive: Prayers by Teenagers. Edited by Carl Koch, St. Mary's Press, Christian Brothers Publications, Winona, MN, 1991.

Faith of Parents, The. Maria Harris, Paulist Press, Mahweh, NJ, 1991.

Apostolic Exhortation on the Family (Familiaris Consortio). John Paul II, United States Catholic Conference, 3211 Fourth Street, NE, Washington, DC 20017-1194, 1984.

Family Perspective in Church and Society: A Manual for All Pastoral Leaders. Ad Hoc Committee on Marriage and Family Life, NCCB, United States Catholic Conference, 3211 Fourth Street, NE, Washington, DC 20017-1194, 1988.

Formidable Energies. Christian Family Movement, P.O. Box 272, Ames, IA 50010, 1988.

I Meet Jesus: He Tells Me "I Love You." Jean Vanier, Paulist Press, Mahweh, NJ, 1982.

I Walk With Jesus. Jean Vanier, Editions Paulines, 250 Boulevard, Saint Francis Nord, Sherbrooke, Q.C., J1E 2B9, Canada.

Making Things Right: The Sacrament of Reconciliation. Jeannine T. Leichner, Our Sunday Visitor, Inc., Huntington, IN 46750, 1980.

Rebuilding the Dream. James Johnson, ed., Christian Family Movement, P.O. Box 272, Ames, IA 50010, 1989.

Saint Joseph's Mass Book. Sister Stephanie Clifford, Collins Liturgical Publishers, 8 Grafton Street, London, England, WIX 3LA.

Saints of the Season for Children. Ethel Marbach, St. Anthony Messenger Press, Cincinnati, 1989.

Seasons of Your Heart: Prayers and Reflections. Macrina Wiederkehr, Harper San Francisco, San Francisco, 1991.

Spirituality of Parenting, The. Maureen Gallagher, Sheed and Ward, Kansas City, MO, 1985.

SPECIAL CONSIDERATIONS IN SHARING FAITH

1. Childcare and Self-care

Today close to eighty-eight percent of all children who return home from school in America will enter a household where every living member has been gone the best ten hours of that day and is now coming home where all the routine business of the household must still be done.

Stephen Glenn and Jane Nelsen
Raising Children for Success

One of the most dramatic changes of the past fifty years is the increasing necessity for parents to entrust the care of their children to persons outside the home and family. Approximately seventy percent of mothers of school-age children are employed full time or part time outside the home. The two-income family is here to stay. Although other family members, such as grandparents, might be willing to help with childcare, many families do not have this luxury.

Parents who work outside the home sometimes lambaste themselves with guilt because of the need to put their children into someone else's care. The children themselves may try to make the parents feel guilty. These parents often try to make up for this supposed neglect with material things or permissiveness.

Guilt is unnecessary and totally nonproductive. When it comes to our family's needs, we do what we have to do. If we simply accept the fact that we work — and don't fuss about it — our children will accept it too and will feel secure. Whether in a single-parent family or a family where both parents work, recognizing the necessity of the situation and maintaining a sensible matter-of-fact approach will make children feel part of the solution, not part of the problem. Children behave best when they feel they are contributing to a working family unit.

Selecting a Childcare Provider

When choosing a childcare provider, consider the following: location, cost, program options, transportation options, staff competency, and health and safety standards. Interview personnel and observe the care facility in operation to ensure that your own philosophy of parenting and your faith perspectives are respected by the staff. In small towns, where fewer options are available, be especially conscience of overcrowding and adequate care. You may decide to look for an at-home care provider who will give your children the kind of care you desire.

If your child has a handicap or special health or social needs, make sure the provider can meet those needs without isolating or embarrassing the child. A childcare provider associated with a church will sometimes provide the extra advantage of nurturing your child's faith in ordinary daily activities.

As the number of families needing childcare increases, more options become available. Day-care homes or centers provide care specifically designed for children's needs. There are also school-based programs. If your child's school does not offer before-school or after-school care, you may want to gather other parents to advocate with school leaders to start a program in your community. Consultation service is usually available to schools who are interested in this option.

Another option is the in-home caregiver that allows children to be at home in their neighborhood after school. It is less structured than a care center. High-school and college students or retired persons make excellent caregivers in this situation.

Families with older grade-school children who do not need constant supervision often make use of recreational programs through YMCA, Scouts, or other private and public agencies. These activities with peers are supervised by adults and avoid the undesirable situation of leaving children without supervision.

Self-care

Childcare experts agree that children are capable of self-care (formerly called latch key) by the time they reach the age of twelve. This depends, of course, on factors such as the child's maturity level and personality, the safety of the neighborhood, and the availability of a trusted adult in case of emergency. Some children may be ready to provide care for their brothers and sisters at home if clear guidelines and support systems are available.

Before you decide on self-care, be certain your children are ready. To help with this process, ask yourself the following questions that are taken from the brochure *Should Your Child Be Home Alone?* developed by Phyllis Chandler of the Family Service Unit of Metropolitan Omaha.

1. How old is my child? (No child of six or seven should be left at home alone, but a thirteen-year-old generally can. A child younger than age twelve should probably not remain at home alone all day on a regular basis.)
2. How much time will my child spend alone? (An hour or two before or after school is very different from an entire day.)
3. How mature is my child? Is he able to occupy himself appropriately, make good decisions, accept responsibility?
4. How does my child feel about being home alone? (Some children feel important, trusted, and "grown up"; others can be frightened and lonely. Talk honestly with your child about his or her feelings.)

5. What basic rules do I expect my child to follow and does she follow them consistently?
6. How safe is our neighborhood? (No one should assume that their neighborhood is completely safe, but some are more safe than others.)
7. Is there an adult always available to my child?
8. Does my child know what to do in an emergency?
9. Will there be other children at home? What exactly are the responsibilities of each child?

There are booklets and minicourses children can use to prepare for the responsibility of self-care. See the resource listing on pages 93-94 for more details.

Grade-school children need to belong, to develop skills that aid in self-esteem, and to be independent. All these needs can be met if self-care is undertaken with a positive and well-prepared approach. Let your children know they are contributing to the family's overall good by being responsible for themselves. Children take great pride in being a contributing part of a working family unit. Positively reinforce all mature actions.

Helpful Hints

The following suggestions from the Family Service Unit of Metropolitan Omaha will make your child's self-care situation a more positive experience for both of you.

Have clear expectations. Talk about what you expect and then write down things so your children will have something to refer to. Establish a few basic rules that cover safety, friends, television, and phone use. Have guidelines for answering the door and other important issues. Remember to build in logical consequences when serious violations occur. Your children's self-esteem and sense of belonging will be enhanced when they see themselves as participants in family decisions rather than victims of a situation beyond their control. Include chores in the schedule. Allow time for fun, music practice, homework, and other favorite activities.

Get feedback. At the end of the day, talk with your child about how the day was spent. Let your child know you are interested. A monthly "check-up" to discuss and affirm the self-care situation can be combined with a special out-to-dinner date or other event.

Be available. Make sure your children know where you are and how to reach you at all times. Leave notes or make phone calls to stay in touch with them when possible. If you cannot be available, arrange for someone else they can contact in case of emergency or if they just need to talk.

Encourage volunteerism. Grade-school children enjoy keeping active and can reap great benefits from involvement in helping others. Helping an elderly neighbor with chores or playing with a small child next-door to relieve the mother might be a great reference for that first job application and will be mutually rewarding.

Studies show that a positive childcare arrangement helps children learn socializing skills. Emphasizing the positive aspects of whatever childcare option you choose will be beneficial to you and your family. Changing childcare providers frequently makes it hard for you and your children to feel secure. Children need a sense of continuity and belonging if they are to accomplish the developmental tasks appropriate for these years. Establishing a relationship of trust and confidence with a caregiver cannot be overemphasized. Faith in God depends largely on the level of trust children have in everyday interactions with those who care for them.

Resources

In Charge: A Complete Handbook for Kids With Working Parents. Kathy S. Kyte. Self-care information for children. For Parents, 8481 North Main Street, Eden, NY 14057.

On My Own: The Kids' Self Care Book. Lynette Long. A self-care course for children ages one through six. Acropolis, Reston, VA, 1984.

Should Your Child Be Home Alone? Phyllis Chandler. Family Services, 2240 Landon Court, Omaha, NE 68102.

When School's Out and Nobody's Home. Peter Coolsen, Michelle Seligson, James Garbarino. National Committee for the Prevention of Child Abuse, 332 South Michigan Avenue, Suite 950, Chicago, IL 60604-4357, 1985.

When You Are in Charge. Developed by Fox Valley Task Force. A workbook to prepare children to be in charge at home. A.A.L., Branch 3729, Appleton, WI 54919.

Working Parent's Guide to Child Care, A. Family Services of Metropolitan Omaha, 2240 Landon Court, Omaha, NE 68102, 1991.

Additional Sources of Information

Project Homesafe. Sponsored by the American Home Economics Association and the Whirlpool Foundation. National Education Advisory Program addressing the issues of latch-key children, Margaret Plantz, project editor, 1-800-252-SAFE.

Other material available from A.I.S. Whirlpool Corporation, P.O. Box 405, St. Joseph, MI 49085.

2. Children and Sunday Worship

"Fifty cents! I'll give fifty cents to anyone who can tell me one important thing they heard in the homily today."

I couldn't believe my ears! My husband was offering to pay our five-year-old, eight-year-old, and ten-year-old for listening to and remembering something from the homily at Mass. This became an on-the-way-home-from-Mass tradition for several years, much against my better judgment. It seemed sacrilegious to me.

But it worked. I could see the growing attentiveness at Mass, even when the celebrant was not energetic and interesting.

These children are now thirteen, sixteen, and nineteen. Over the years, they've grumbled, refused to dress appropriately, and complained openly when holy days backed up on weekends, but they still go regularly to Mass and they still comment on the homily.

Mother of three

Between the ages of nine and fourteen, children may lose the interest and enthusiasm they had when they celebrated first Communion. There may come Sunday mornings when you almost wonder if it's worth going through the hassle of piling everyone in the car and dealing with kids who are half-dressed, angry, and whining. This is fairly common. Welcome to the grade-school years!

It may be comforting for parents to know that children in these years of rapid development will fidget, daydream, "knit" (kneel and sit in alternating rhythm), and slouch at Mass. This is normal for children at this stage of faith development. They may stop singing when hormones cause voice changes, and they may complain that Mass is *boring,* a key adjective for a lot of things during this stage of development.

This section explores the meaning of the Mass and offers practical ways to make Sunday worship a faith-enriching experience for your family as your children move through these challenging years.

Your Child's Experience of Faith

James Fowler describes the faith of the grade-school child as "mythical-literal" faith. Children enter a very critical period on the faith journey shortly after they celebrate their first Communion. They begin to recognize deep-down inside — though they may not be able to verbalize it — that they belong to a unique community. They begin to claim as their own the stories, beliefs, and actions that the community holds dear. Though they may look like they live on another planet, they are closely observing and adopting attitudes of adults around them. Although they seem to be completely absorbed with their peers during this time, children note the authority and example set by the adults in their lives.

Grade-school children may show increased interest in the ritual surrounding the Eucharist, especially if they can get involved in the choir or be an altar server. They may even become the not-so-gentle conscience for parents when it comes to church rules or attendance.

Behavior and words are not good gages for the effectiveness of our faith-sharing efforts at this time. Remember: although children in intermediate grades may begin to look like little adults, they still think like children.

From ages seven to ten, children understand and appreciate the physical and external features of the building and the people surrounding Sunday worship. At the age of eleven or twelve they can begin to understand the spiritual function and meaning of the Mass.

The Mass

The Second Vatican Council changed the language we use to describe our Catholic rituals and beliefs. Rather than attending Mass, the emphasis is now on participation. Father is the celebrant rather than just the person saying Mass. These changes encourage our personal involvement in the wondrous mystery of Jesus' gift of himself in the bread and wine.

The understanding of our community act of worship as an act of thanksgiving and praise sets the tone for how we can teach our children the importance of being faithful to Sunday worship. The word *eucharist* comes from the Greek word meaning "thanksgiving."

As children, we may have gone to church out of obligation or fear of hell. Today, our children can be more positive. When children ask why they have to go to church on Sunday, we can answer, "To give thanks and praise to God with all the other people in our church." We can explain how we give thanks because God has given us everything we have: our lives, our health, our family, our friends, and loved ones. We celebrate Eucharist as a way of being thankful together.

If this sounds simplistic, it is. As our faith matures, we begin to understand that by taking part in the eucharistic celebration, we share in the death and resurrection of Christ by means of this sacred meal. It is an event where Christ is truly present to us, within us individually and as a community. We are nourished and strengthened by the body and blood of Christ, which appears as a small wafer of bread.

Your Child and Mass

This great sacrament puts us in touch with the mystery of God's infinite love for us and Christ's continued presence in the bread and wine, in the sacred Scriptures, and in the human community gathered for worship. All of this is true. Our children will learn this in their religion classes, and it is good for us to reinforce these truths.

Explaining theology to children, however, will not motivate them to go to church. The spirit in which you gather up your family on Sunday and the attitude you convey to your children as to why *you* go to Mass will speak louder and clearer than theological truths.

The Eucharist is an opportunity to learn more about your faith through the Scriptures and the homily. Catholic beliefs are laid out before us during the Mass: the Trinity, the Incarnation, the death and resurrection of Jesus, the communion of saints, the presence of the Holy Spirit. All are celebrated in this central act of worship. You can experience the presence of Jesus and enjoy a sense of belonging to a community that is itself the Body of Christ on earth.

Your own understanding of the eucharistic celebration and your expressed personal desire to worship as a community will influence your children the most.

You and Mass

We all have different relationships with the Church. Some of us, for example, have been away from the practice of faith and Sunday Mass — but the Lord works in mysterious ways. A child's first Communion or confirmation is a time when the Church warmly welcomes everyone. Adults returning to practice the faith will want to find "grown-up" information about the Mass to build upon the elementary understanding gained years ago. Such material is mentioned in the resource listing on pages 101-102. If these resources are shared with children, everyone's appreciation for the meaning of the Eucharist is enriched.

Some parents are in an interfaith marriage or don't worship as a couple and family. Spouses cannot force each other to worship. Jesus' approach would be a loving and consistent invitation. Following that example will decrease conflict and anxiety surrounding family worship time. Pray together at home and avoid alliances of one parent and child against the other parent. Involving children in heated arguments about worship serves no positive purpose and can be destructive to their faith development — not to mention the damage it does to the marriage.

Some parents have been Catholic their entire lives and have strong feelings about their children attending Mass every Sunday. Children's complaints and questions about going to church are especially disturbing to these parents. It is not productive to make church attendance a battleground. Parents who engage in heated exchanges and use threats to manipulate their children defeat the purpose of a eucharistic celebration. Firmly state that going to church is not a negotiable house rule; eventually, the teenagers will grudgingly accept the fact.

Listen patiently to your child's complaints; accept their feelings. You might even say, "I sometimes felt that way when I was young, too." If they feel they've been listened to and understood, children will see that your house rule about going to church is as a benevolent one.

When children reach junior high, give them some control of the situation; give them some options. Allow them to choose when they want to go to Mass, which liturgy is most agreeable to them. Giving them a choice will alleviate some of the tension. If it doesn't, don't despair. The tension surrounding adolescent behavior is a result of movement from one level of faith to a deeper, more mature level.

When your children enter early adolescence, their understanding of the Eucharist will change and begin to reflect their increasing ability to appreciate symbol and ritual. John Westerhoff, a noted religious educator, calls the faith of children of this age "affiliative" faith. Your children's faith meets their need for belonging to a community — and their faith is shaped by the community in which they live and worship.

Religious focus during this time is based on feelings more than concepts. Westerhoff calls this a religion of the heart rather than the head. Providing opportunities for good Sunday liturgy and meaningful worship in a place where children will see their peers and feel at home is important for their faith formation, even if they resist.

Helpful Hints

On the average, you will spend twenty-five years getting children off to church. The following suggestions are from a parent who has faithfully moved a houseful of children from bed to pew for thirteen hundred consecutive Sundays. They may be helpful to you.

Prepare ahead of time. The night before or several hours before Mass, make sure clothing is ready for quick dressing without hassles. Locate prayer books and other items the children may want to take with them. Before bed the night before, you may want to read the Sunday Scriptures as a family.

Celebrate with meaning. Make celebrating Eucharist a family affair whenever possible. Make use of parish preschool programs for wiggly youngsters so you can attend to older children without distraction.

Discipline with love. If correcting children in church is necessary, do it lovingly with a hug or a gentle word. Never humiliate a child with a sharp correction or use words such as "shut up" or "you'll get it at home if you don't...."

Sit in front. Give younger children Mass books so they can follow what is happening and participate fully. Point out the important parts of Mass. Sitting in front helps everyone's concentration.

Keep the celebration going. Reinforce good behavior by surprising children with a trip to the doughnut shop after Mass. Let a different child choose the breakfast menu each week. This adds to the feeling of celebration.

Select a familiar community. Worship in a community where children will meet and greet friends regularly at Mass.

Good manners is good enough. Don't expect perfect posture or attention at Mass. When you don't see reverence, be satisfied with good manners.

Encourage direct involvement. Encourage your children to become altar servers or members of the choir. A word of caution: don't let Sunday responsibilities split your family. If you lector and your children are involved in other ways, coordinate your schedules. If this isn't possible, you may want to give up your liturgical ministry for a few years to keep the family together.

Emphasize the positive. Affirm your children's active participation and attentiveness at church by telling them the positive behavior you observe. "Catch" them doing things right rather than criticizing them for doing things wrong.

Maintain a pleasant atmosphere. Don't argue on the way to church. You may want to observe silence and ask children to sit quietly and think about what they will want to offer to God at this Mass as well as what they may want to give thanks for.

Build community before going to church. Let your children bring friends to church with them. Take a neighbor, grandparent, or friend from another church.

Resources

Called to His Supper. Preparation for first Communion, Jeannine T. Leichner, Our Sunday Visitor, Huntington, IN, 1990.

Come Worship With Us: Explaining the Mass. Frank Buckley, Liguori Publications, Liguori, MO, 1987.

How the Mass Came to Be: From the Last Supper to Today's Eucharist. Pierre Loret, C.SS.R., Liguori Publications, Liguori, MO, 1985.

Joy, Joy, the Mass: Our Family Celebration. Jeannine T. Leichner, Our Sunday Visitor, Huntington, IN, 1978.

Mass for Children, The. H.J. Richards, Liturgical Press, Collegeville, MN, 1991.

My Beginning Mass Book. JoAnn M. Angers, Twenty-Third Publications, Mystic, CT, 1978.

Sunday Mass: What Part Do You Play? Robert Rietcheck, C.SS.R., and Daniel Korn, C.SS.R., Liguori Publications, Liguori, MO, 1985.

This Is Our Mass. Thomas Coyle, Twenty-Third Publications, Mystic, CT, 1989.

Understanding the Mass. Archbishop Daniel E. Pilarczyk, Our Sunday Visitor, Huntington, IN, 1987.

3. Children With Disabilities

It was an ordinary Sunday morning at Mass. Our family was squeezed into one long pew toward the front of church.

Then something extraordinary happened. Michael asked, "When do I get to go get Jesus?" There was nothing very profound about the question, but the fact that Michael was born with Down's syndrome made it a very important question for us. Why not? Michael just happened to be seven years old, the appropriate age for most Catholic children to celebrate their first Communion.

That question made us aware of how much Michael had observed and learned from watching his siblings. This was the stirring of his first introduction into special-education classes which prepared him for the sacrament within a year. By the time his second-grade sister was ready for her first Communion, Michael was also ready to "go get Jesus!"

Rosemary Wais
Mother of Michael

At the heart of our Christian tradition is the belief that every human being is fashioned in the image of God and that God loves each person, without exception and without condition.

By the time Michael was seven years old, his parents, family, and friends had accepted and adapted to his disability. They could see the goodness and special giftedness in Michael, even amidst daily frustrations.

In countless ordinary ways, Michael's family loved him unconditionally. They cared for him, satisfied his needs, and encouraged him. He knew himself loved, not for his accomplishments or the great love he gives others. He knew himself loved because he is God's creation.

To the degree that we love and care for our children and see their immanent goodness, we share faith in the most essential and effective way.

Your Child's Needs

As children progress from age seven to fourteen, new challenges will arise. They do not progress developmentally in the same way; they grow and develop in their own unique ways according to their individual abilities. Although they may have special physical and emotional needs, all children share a common need for a relationship with God. This need might differ in expression because of a child's limitations, but it is essentially the same need.

The categories "trainable" and "educable" refer more to academic instruction than to faith growth. All children with disabilities can understand that they are loved by God, that they are good and gifted in a unique way. They can understand the friendship of Jesus and his special care for them.

The unique set of circumstances that confront you as a parent will determine how you share faith with your child on a day-to-day basis. Parents of children with disabilities find that mental development is not necessarily proportionate to spiritual capacity and that Christianity may be grasped at many levels. The depth of their own child's simple faith or struggle with faith is an example and inspiration to them and their families.

Between the ages of seven and fourteen, most children distinguish good from evil to some degree. Thus, they need instruction to help shape their decisions. A strong sense of their own self-worth, necessary for overcoming obstacles and fully using their capacities, is important. As the number of contacts outside their home increases, they need a sense of belonging; they need clear guidelines for relationships with others.

Christian faith provides a foundation for healthy self-esteem, decision-making, and relating to others. As a child moves through this period and into early adulthood, a solid belief in God and the company of Jesus can help in facing the challenges ahead.

What Can You Do?

Your child learns about God and your faith traditions at home. In addition to the ordinary ways of sharing faith, your child can benefit from involvement in a parish or diocesan special religious-education class. Ask your parish or diocesan religious-education office about the availability of sacramental-preparation programs for children with special learning needs. If none is available, you are the most effective advocate for your child in this matter. Every child deserves the opportunity to celebrate fully in the sacraments of penance, holy Communion, and confirmation. Excellent resource materials for teachers and parents are available. Two of those are mentioned in the resource listing on page 109.

In some areas of the country, several churches cooperate in hiring or training a special-education teacher who can serve families from a large area. Nationally, many creative efforts are taking place.

Religious-education Classes

According to experienced educators, the sole criterion of acceptance in a religious-education program is the child's capacity to be present to another and the parents' desire to share this experience with them.

When a child has severe disabilities, parents' energies and concerns are often totally taken up with day-to-day needs; little energy may be left for the child's spiritual development. Prayer, listening to God's Word, and church attendance may seem like luxuries when braces, feeding tubes, and medications are a constant challenge. Yet, parents who attend to the spiritual growth of their family have increased energy for the daily task of parenting. Even vocational trainers who do job placement of adults with disabilities claim that the personal qualities of honesty and kindness that develop out of a faith formation are as important as job skills in an individual's overall success.

Celebrating the Sacraments

Though much of your child's religious instruction may need to be given on a one-to-one basis, a religious-education program gives your child a chance to celebrate faith with peers. Whether your child attends sessions in the general religious-education program or has special classes, the lively faith of other children plays a crucial role. Your child needs to observe peers celebrating the sacraments of penance, holy Communion, and confirmation. These sacramental celebrations are community rituals available to all. They enrich all members of the baptized community.

First Communion: Michael's case is not unusual. Children who have experienced prayer and a Christian environment at home as well as worship with a parish community will probably be curious about and eager for celebrating first Communion. Celebrating holy communion with family and friends gives children an experience of belonging and being like others in the family and Church. What children actually grasp intellectually about the Eucharist as the body and blood of Christ is secondary to their experience of receiving Jesus and being part of a believing community.

The best preparation for this sacrament is the use of concrete symbols. Liturgical prayers, songs, and acted-out stories teach children about Jesus and the Eucharist. Formally, this process takes about a year. There are excellent materials especially designed for use by children with disabilities. They stress belonging, caring, and sharing meals with others. Preparation will include some understanding of the life and the person of Jesus, the distinction between eucharistic bread and ordinary bread, and the importance of a desire to receive Jesus. Children with severe mental disabilities may not grasp any of this. Still, the faith of the family or friends is sufficient for celebrating the sacrament with proper authority's consent; that is, religion teacher, priest, or deacon.

It is your responsibility — with input from your pastor — to decide when and how first Communion takes place. It can be celebrated with just the immediate family, at a Sunday parish Mass, or in conjunction with the first Communion of other children.

Reconciliation: In preparing to celebrate the sacrament of penance with children with disabilities, the emphasis is on the positive aspects of the unfailing love and mercy of God. Teachers and materials avoid instilling feelings of guilt or negative attitudes toward self or God. In many cases, children with disabilities celebrate their first Communion before celebrating reconciliation. Your child will likely be prepared separately for these two sacraments.

There is no definite age for reconciliation. Your child's ability to distinguish right from wrong, awareness of trust in Jesus' forgiving love, and an ability to express sorrow are evidence of preparedness. Your child's preparation for this special event begins at home. Experiences of God's forgiveness from you and others are key elements in understanding the meaning of the sacrament. The special-education teacher will help you determine when and how to celebrate this sacrament. You may wish to have your child's first reconciliation at home or in the reconciliation room at church. Your cooperation in preparing your child will make these decisions much easier.

Confirmation: Like baptism, confirmation is a sacrament of initiation into the Body of Christ. The focus of your child's preparation for this sacrament will be an understanding or feeling for the power of the Holy Spirit, personally and in the life of the larger community. The sacrament's rich symbols of fire, water, and oil are understood and appreciated at different levels according to each child's capacities.

Your child, like all God's creation, has been given gifts and qualities that can serve your family and the community. Confirmation recognizes these personal gifts and affirms their value. In very quiet ways, you may have seen your child transform others and evoke from them generosity, goodness, and compassion. In simple ways, your child can understand gifts of the Holy Spirit like fortitude, wisdom, and reverence. As with other sacraments, theology is not the key issue. Rather, the focus is on experiencing the power of God's Spirit.

There are many creative ways to explain the truths of the faith to your children. One parent of a Down's syndrome child described the Holy Spirit this way: "Peel an apple. The outer skin is the protector, like God the Father. The part of the apple we eat, the flesh, is like the Jesus bread we eat at Mass: God the Son. The seed, the core, is like the seed planted in us at baptism. When we are confirmed, that little seed grows in our hearts to make us stronger and more loving Christians. This is like God the Holy Spirit."

It is important for us not to judge our children's readiness for formal religious education or the sacraments by their behavior alone. The way they behave during these growing years may not reflect their spiritual maturity. The sacraments are not rewards for virtue; they are channels of grace that help us and our children move closer to God. They are moments when God touches all of our lives and strengthens us for our journey. Sacraments are like windows through which we see God's face and feel God's healing touch. The sacraments are the community's celebration of God's presence in each individual and the Church as a whole. With this in mind, we approach the Church and ask for help in preparing our children for the sacraments of penance, holy Communion, and confirmation.

Helpful Hints

Here are some helpful guidelines for families who have children with disabilities.

Rely on other parents. One of the best forms of support comes from other parents who have been or are currently in similar situations. Organizations of such parents exist in most communities. People in rural areas may need to travel to the nearest large community to find these organizations. Seek them out and make use of them, for your own good and the good of your child. Medical, educational, and psychological support services are readily available in many places. Some of these are mentioned in the resource listing on page 109.

Gather with other parents like yourself. Become a strong advocate with your Church for special-education programs, accessible buildings, homilies, and educational opportunities that are sensitive to families affected by physical, developmental, or emotional disabilities.

Pray. Your own home is the first church your child will experience, the primary place your child encounters a forgiving, generous, and powerful God.

Pray daily with your child. Bless your child. Read simple stories about Jesus and those who love him and his friends. Display religious art and objects in your home that remind your entire family of God's love and presence. Use the seasons of Advent-Christmas and Lent-Easter to celebrate in concrete ways how much we have been loved by God throughout history.

Discipline. Discipline your child to show that you care. Discipline is your way of saying that you care enough about your child's future to set limits. Avoid smothering your child. Your child does not need protection or rescue. Your child needs to learn from experiencing consequences of actions chosen. When possible, assign certain tasks and responsibilities relative to your child's abilities. This builds your child's confidence and reinforces a sense of being a contributing member of the family.

Parents who accept children as they are help fashion their children into individuals who can accept themselves. Don't let your children develop the idea that God is responsible for any limitations. Rather, help your children turn to God for strength in overcoming obstacles.

Resources

Exceptional Parents Magazine. Box 3000, Dept. E.P., Denville, NJ 97834.

Impact of Chronic Illness on Psychosocial Stages of Human Development, The. Available through the National Center for Education in Maternal Child Health, 38th & R Streets, NW, Washington, DC 20057.

Additional Sources of Information

TAPP Central Office. Federation for Children with Special Needs, 95 Berkeley Street, Suite 104, Boston, MA 02116. (Parent training and information projects available in most states. To obtain the name of the center nearest you, contact this address.)

4. Discipline

Enjoy your children, and let them grow. Let them develop their own peculiar quirks. They will anyway. So you might as well smile occasionally and enjoy the process.

Rev. Robert Meyering
What To Do When You Can't Do It All

Several months after taking a course in parenting and putting the skills to use in his own household, a father of seven testified to the "magical change" in his household when a negative atmosphere was changed to a positive one. With a bemused smile, he said, "I just never realized that parenting could be fun."

Our children are God's gift to us, but they do not come with a book of instructions. Learning how to parent, which means learning how to be an effective disciplinarian, can make the difference between enjoying our children's peculiar quirks and allowing them to drive us bonkers.

The close similarity between the word *disciple* and the word *discipline* is not accidental. The word *disciple* refers to a person who is a follower, a believer in the thought and teachings of a leader. The word *discipline* means to train, educate, or guide another person.

Every Christian parent has the task of disciple-making. In a sense, God loans our children to us for a short time. To lead children effectively to become disciples of Jesus Christ, we need a consistent, loving method of discipline. By developing that consistent, loving method of discipline, we become effective leaders.

Children who are disciplined in a loving atmosphere learn to believe in themselves, know what they should do, and freely choose to do it. They are disciplined in an atmosphere of positive expectations. They learn respect for their parents, for themselves, for others, and for the world around them.

Undisciplined children cannot choose to sit still or to take turns, let alone follow the Ten Commandments. Without lovingly set and consistently enforced limitations, children's capacities for self-control and free choice are seriously limited. Undisciplined persons cannot choose freely; they are controlled by others or by their own need for immediate satisfaction.

The capacity to learn self-control and free choice is a gift present at birth that develops rapidly between the ages of seven and fourteen. As children progress through these ages, they gain the ability to understand and to choose right from wrong. As our children make the changes, we need to adjust our methods of discipline.

The Nature of Discipline

Discipline is more than a method of setting limits. Discipline is necessary for personality development and healthy self-esteem. Discipline helps children develop moral standards and security. If we want our children to be courageous, cooperative, and responsible members of society, we will need to train them, guide them, and discipline them. If we want faith-filled followers of Christ, we need to lead our children in ways of discipleship.

Bookstores and libraries offer information on philosophies and methods of disciplining children. They include topics like effective parenting, active parenting, realistic and democratic parenting, disciplining with purpose, disciplining with love, and positive discipline. What you believe and how you discipline may come from materials you've read or lectures you've heard or even from other parents' advice.

Yet, most parents discipline children out of their own experiences of childhood. Parents tend to unconsciously repeat what their parents did. To quote one young mother, "I yelled at my kids this morning and heard my own mother coming out of my mouth!" Sometimes, people parent in a way completely opposite the style their own parents use, as a reaction to their family-of-origin experience.

That can be good — but it can also be not so good. Appropriate ways to discipline can be learned, just as inappropriate ones can be unlearned. It's not easy, but it is possible. Problems in a family can often be directly attributed to ineffective discipline. In this section, we will share ideas about discipline that many parents have found effective.

Discipline and the Stages of Development

The goal of discipline is to help children use their free will as God intended. The way we discipline should take into consideration our children's changing capacity to make decisions. A child of twelve or fourteen, for example, is capable of moral reasoning at a level the seven-year-old cannot. Children move from one stage of moral maturity to another by building upon what they already know and by being challenged to the next level of maturity.

Children between the ages of seven and fourteen are egocentric. They choose to do what is best for themselves according to their own needs and surroundings. Discipline should take that into consideration.

As children mature, they become less egocentric. The fourteen-year-old is capable of concern for others, more so than the seven-year-old. As leaders in the home, parents can share their own beliefs and motivations, even with younger children who cannot fully understand them. Children need to be consistently challenged toward more mature behaviors.

Your children's ability to make good moral judgments about their own and others' behavior is a skill that develops as they move from childhood into adulthood. In the earliest stage, children choose right from wrong simply because they fear punishment. They are motivated by hope of reward or fear of punishment. Some adults are stuck at this level of moral development, which is unfortunate for society and the Church.

At the next stage, children conform to the wishes of those in authority because they want a specific reward. They are still basically motivated by self-interest, but this behavior is not immature and selfish. It is age-appropriate and a necessary step in the maturing process. It is not appropriate to punish children of this age for their enlightened self-interest, but it is good to point them toward a higher motivation.

If we consistently approve good behavior and enforce consequences for unacceptable behavior, our children eventually learn that living according to certain principles and beliefs brings approval. Children need and want adult approval, and so in the next stage, they will obey to win praise or affirmation from parents and other authority figures.

As we discipline our children through these stages, we can depend on others to reinforce their moral growth; we are not alone. Teachers, Scout leaders, coaches, and childcare providers should know our concerns and values regarding our children's maturation process. These people can be valuable sources of support for us and mentors to our children.

When our children become teenagers and young adults, they will be increasingly aware of the social implications of their actions. They will recognize and respect the rights of others and the demands of justice. Their choices will be made according to principles instead of relying solely on feelings and desires. Many of us are still working through this level of moral maturity.

Helpful Hints

There are no perfect parents; there are no perfect children. Parenting is a vocation — a call from God — to give, nurture, and protect human life. Some days we are good at it. Some days we aren't. Ideally, discipline is the way we guide and train our children according to our own beliefs and values. Yet, on a day-to-day basis, discipline is often simply the way we react according to how we feel at the time. Our actions reflect little of what we really believe.

Disciplining according to our values, however, is important.

Discipline based on values helps us lead our children toward a trust in God. The following suggestions from experienced parents may be of help.

Choose a balanced parenting style. Don't be too rigid or too permissive. Punitive parenting thwarts a child's development, creativity, and decision-making abilities. Permissiveness renders a child unable to exercise self-discipline and self-control. Both extremes destroy free will, which is the child's God-given gift for discovering his potential.

Remember the goal of parental discipline. That goal is to raise self-disciplined children. Neither society nor Church values behavior that is constantly controlled by external laws. Persons who have the strength of their convictions and are responsible for themselves make solid citizens and effective disciples.

Set clear limits. Set limits regarding your children's behavior, appropriate to their age and their development. Make sure your children understand what those limits are and why they exist. Limits and consequences should be adjusted as your children mature.

Permit your child to learn from natural consequences. Natural consequences are those that occur naturally from an action without parental intervention. Allowing children the privilege of experiencing the consequences of their own actions, if those consequences aren't life threatening, is a tremendous educational tool. For instance, if a child refuses to eat a meal and you allow that child to experience hunger before the next meal, he will learn to eat at mealtime. If a child uses her allowance foolishly and then doesn't have money for something she really wants (and you don't give in and give her money), she's likely to learn not to use her allowance foolishly.

Allowing children to experience the natural consequences of their actions means letting them learn from their own mistakes. The best gift you can give your children is to help them understand that mistakes are learning experiences. Most seven-year-olds are capable of understanding cause and effect. If your child leaves his school uniform under a pile of books overnight and you do not allow him to wear it in that condition, he will get a demerit. He will also learn to hang up his uniform. If you rescue him by pressing it, he will learn that taking care of his clothes isn't necessary, because you'll do it. Rescuing children robs them of the opportunity to learn from their mistakes and to become self-sufficient adults.

Provide logical consequences. Logical consequences are the ones parents deliberately enforce to show children what logically follows when they violate family rules. Taking a bike out after dark without permission might result in losing the privilege of riding the bike for a week. Not studying for a test might result in enforcing special study time and the loss of TV privileges.

Be consistent without being rigid. Consistency gives children a sense of security and the sure knowledge that their parents care about them. They know what's expected of them and what the consequences will be if those expectations are not met. Flexibility allows children to develop listening, thinking, and negotiating skills. Rigidity destroys human relationships and refuses to recognize the uniqueness of each child and the variety of human circumstances. Children shouldn't always have their way, but they should be allowed, within reason, to have their say. There is a time when parents need to say, without discussion, "You'll do this because I know what's best for you right now."

Include your child in decision-making whenever possible. Give your children some choice and responsibility in deciding on house rules or personal schedules. It builds self-confidence and encourages self-discipline. Family meetings are an excellent way to include children in setting house rules about television, study time, and other daily matters. By age seven, a child can help choose time, frequency, and the agenda for family meetings. Parents do not abdicate their leadership by using these methods; rather, they share their leadership with children in a way that builds mutual respect and responsibility for self.

Be positive. Affirm good behavior. "Catch" your children doing things that are good. Value your children as individuals, appreciating their uniqueness and individual "peculiar quirks." Concentrate on improvement, not perfection, and give positive strokes for small steps. Remember: children will not do what does not work.

Respect your child's unique personality and abilities. Each of your children will respond differently to your methods of discipline. What works for one may not work for another. Position in the family, personality, and level of maturity differ for each child. A sociable and active child who loves to talk on the phone may need a different set of rules about completing homework at night than a quiet, shy child whose favorite pastime is reading.

These are only a few of the many helpful insights about discipline that can be learned from experienced parents and family counselors. There are many more. Rapid sociological changes are taking place in this century. Family relationships have undergone radical changes. Formerly, extended families used to take part in the rearing of children. Now, the nuclear family carries the primary responsibility. Parents need all the help they can get to raise their family in this fast-moving, technological society. Many resources are available. Several are mentioned in the resource listing below.

Because our children are basically good and simple — and a constant challenge — they have the power to lead us to God. We are, therefore, disciples to one another in our homes.

Resources

Active Parenting: Teaching Courage, Cooperation and Responsibility. Michael J. Popkin, HarperCollins, New York, 1987.

Between Parent and Child. Haim G. Ginott, Avon Books, New York, 1976.

Between Parent and Teenager. Haim G. Ginott, Avon Books, New York, 1982.

Dare to Discipline (rev. ed.), James Dobson, Tyndale, Wheaton, IL, 1991.

Discipline With Purpose Workbook. Vasiloff and Lenz, 2547 North 61 Street, Omaha, NE 68104, 1989.

Family Enrichment, Understanding Us. Patrick J. Carnes, Interpersonal Communication Programs, Inc., 7201 South Broadway, Littleton, CO 80122, 1981.

Making Children Mind Without Losing Yours. Kevin Leman, Revell, Tarrytown, NY, 1983.

Parent Power! A Common-Sense Approach to Parenting in the '90's and Beyond. John Rosemond, Andrews and McMeel Publishers, Kansas City, MO, 1991.

Parents and Discipline. Herbert Wagemaker, Jr. Westminster/John Knox Press, Louisville, 1980.

P.E.T. Parent Effectiveness Training: The Tested New Way to Raise Responsible Children. Dr. Thomas Gordon, a Plume Book, New American Library, Times Mirror, New York, London, Scarborough, Ontario, 1970.

Power of a Parent's Words. H. Norman Wright, Regal Books, division of G.L. Publications, Ventura, CA, 1991.

Practical Parenting Tips for the School Age Years. Vicki Lansky, Bantam Books, New York, 1985.

What's a Kid To Do? Practicing Moral Decision-Making With 10- to 13-Year-Olds. John A. Flanagan, St. Anthony Messenger Press, Cincinnati, 1986.

5. Ecumenical Families

If you identify the aspects of faith that you have in common and reflect these shared faith values, your child will come to know God through your love.

Phyllis Chandler and Joan Burney
Sharing the Faith With Your Child
(From Birth to Age Six)

Through the ages, hearts and imaginations have been captivated by love stories bringing together a woman and a man who have different backgrounds and beliefs. Theater patrons and readers have cheered the lovers on, wanting them to get together and wishing them happiness.

In real life, love stories are all around us. The number of Catholics who marry persons from other Christian and non-Christian religions increases every year. This trend has ushered families into an exciting and challenging period of ecumenism never dreamed of thirty-five years ago.

Ecumenical families have a special opportunity to bring about what Christ desired for all of us: unity among believers. The domestic church — the church of the home — may hold the key to accomplishing this unity and thus pave the way for organized religion to overcome barriers.

Unlike stories of romantic fiction that end with a dramatic denouement, real-life couples must deal with "the rest of the story," when the white-hot fire of romantic love turns into the glowing embers of a working love relationship. The arrival of children, blessings though they are, puts the whole picture into a different and more challenging focus.

Support

In the past, the Catholic Church seriously frowned upon what used to be called "mixed marriages." The papal encyclical *Apos-*

tolic Exhortation on the Family (Familiaris Consortio) issued in 1981, however, reflects a positive change in the Church's attitude. For the first time, official Church teaching affirmingly linked the sacramental life of the family with Christianity in ecumenical families.

Though there are substantial challenges to the emerging generation of interfaith families, the possibilities for a rich interchange of traditions are also present. This is especially true in the church of the home, where parents shape the unique faith that is passed on to their children.

Though a variety of terms are used for couples that blend two religious traditions in their marriage, this chapter uses the term *ecumenical,* applying it to couples blending two Christian traditions in one home.

If your children are growing up in an ecumenical family, new tensions may arise as your children reach school age. By seven or eight, decisions will need to be made about school or religious-education programs and about the preparation for the sacraments of reconciliation and first Communion.

Now is the time to decide in which specific religious tradition your children will be raised. Perhaps you delayed making a choice because of family tensions surrounding the baptisms of your children. That choice can no longer be delayed. Children between the ages of seven and fourteen need to belong. Become an active part of a church community in which your children can share faith with their peers — always remembering that there are no perfect parishes. If your parish does not have a sensitivity to your special concerns, talk to the pastoral staff about what can be done to make ecumenical families more welcome and comfortable.

The primary concern in pastoral care of ecumenical families is no longer to convert the partner who is not Catholic. Rather, pastoral care is directed toward helping the couple share their faith, achieve unity in their relationship with God and community, and enrich their own spirituality.

Most first Communion programs have a parent-participation component that teaches parents how to share faith beliefs. If your child has not been baptized, you can participate in a baptismal-preparation process. Some parishes have a Rite of Christian Initiation of Children (RCIC) and other programs that ignite the faith of parents as well as children. If a spouse who is not Catholic is interested in full membership in the Catholic Church, the Rite of Christian Initiation of Adults (RCIA) is an enriching experience available in many parishes.

Helpful Hints

The faith passed on to children is a unique blend of each parent's Church teaching and personal spirituality. It is important to remember that faith is not simply a set of teachings; it is an orientation of the heart toward Jesus Christ. The hallmark of a person of faith is not only knowledge of doctrine but a love of God and love of others as well.

The following suggestions come from parents who are of different Christian traditions but are committed to passing on one and the same deep faith in God to their children.

Pray together as a couple and as a family. Some individuals find this particularly difficult. Perhaps a few moments of silent prayer together as a couple can be a starting point. Mealtime, bedtime, and special days are natural times of prayer. Decide as a couple if you will use formal or spontaneous prayer. Ecumenical couples pass on faith by nurturing their own faith.

Accentuate the positive. Your attitude toward God and organized religion is an essential factor in your children's faith development. Detailed aspects of religious teachings and rules mean very little to children until they develop abstract-thinking ability around the age of twelve or thirteen.

Instead, recognize and share your positive common beliefs and rituals. Emphasize the richness of what you share, like the belief in God's compassion and forgiveness, or a trust in the power of the Holy Spirit.

You may share a personal knowledge of Jesus as savior or friend. Perhaps your common sharing point will be Scripture stories that demonstrate Jesus' love of the poor, or the great commandment to love one another. Some couples list the common treasures they want their children to inherit, a sort of spiritual will. Accentuate beliefs or traditions you agree upon. Many parents are surprised to find that their common ground is much larger than they thought.

Eliminate the negative. Some areas of faith and practice of religion cause tension and disagreement within ecumenical families. There is no way to eliminate that tension entirely. You did not create doctrinal differences; you inherited them. But how you respond to these differences in the presence of your children will deeply influence each child's faith.

Experienced interfaith parents caution against arguing about matters of faith and religion in front of children. Disagreements should be discussed in private or with other adults. Your energies need to focus on mutual understanding: exactly what are the differences?

The Association of Interchurch Families cautions against by-passing matters of religion entirely to avoid friction. Silence does not help you or your children. You cannot eliminate differences in faith traditions, but you can eliminate the conflicts over those differences that have a negative impact on everyone's faith life.

Choose religious education and church affiliation based on mutual compromise. Studies indicate that if both parents regularly attended church with their children, the children remain in the church as adults. The laissez-faire approach of "letting children choose for themselves" when they get older almost always leads to the children making no choice at all.

Your example is important. Though family traditions and rituals have a formative effect on your children's faith formation, worshiping and affiliating with a faith community are necessary to sustain the family in times of crisis and transition and to challenge the faith of the family to growth.

Not all ecumenical marriages are the same. Some are between two persons who are strongly committed to their own individual denominations. Some marriages have one partner strongly committed and one who remains on the fence. In some marriages, neither spouse has a strong feeling or commitment about church attendance. Even when two Catholics marry, their experience of Catholicism may be so different that they are miles apart in passing on common aspects of faith to their children.

Whatever decision you make about church attendance, take into consideration the needs of every member of your family. Disregarding this sensitivity results in tension that will negatively influence your children's images of God and of Church. Some couples find that a third party or an ecumenical support community can aid them in these difficult decisions.

Respect your child's ability to understand denominational differences. One of the most painful times for ecumenical families can be the time of first Communion. Though Christian churches mutually recognize the validity of one another's baptism (with some exceptions), they do not recognize the other sacraments of initiation: Eucharist and confirmation.

Children are confused when one of you is excluded from receiving Communion because you're not in "full communion" with the Church. They're not capable of the abstract thinking required for understanding denominational teachings. They are incapable of understanding the concepts behind our belief in the Real Presence of Christ in the Eucharist.

Your role at this time is to emphasize the love of Jesus for them and the unique gift Jesus gives in holy Communion. It is not appropriate or helpful to discuss the difference between transubstantiation and transignification or how denominations differ on this. Answer questions as simply as possible. One father's response when Mommy could not receive Communion was direct and personal: "I do not understand why Mommy can't receive Jesus today. It is a problem our churches have to straighten out."

At confirmation, the situation is more complicated. By age thirteen or fourteen, children are able to clarify information and interpret data more effectively. They can discuss differences in belief and practices. Your own example in discussing and negotiating differences will have the greatest impact on your children at this age level. They may have many unanswerable questions. Listen attentively to these questions and teach your children the importance of discovering the answers together.

Meal prayers, night prayers, holiday celebrations, and praying Scripture together lay a solid spiritual base for early adolescents in the midst of this questioning. Encourage your children to participate in church youth activities and service projects with others their age. Gather for prayer and celebration with other families who have early adolescents.

Join other ecumenical families in the struggle. In the last ten years, there has been an increasing number of parish, national, and international movements and groups founded by ecumenical families. These groups bring couples and parents together for dialogue on difficult issues and to share practical solutions. Each one's ability to rise above "denominational" differences is encouragement for all others. These groups produce newsletters, books, and tapes on cutting-edge issues in ecumenical households. Some of these are mentioned in the following resource listing.

Resources

Centerpiece. Newsletter of the Association of Interchurch Families, No. 14 Winter, 1985-86. The Old Bakery, Donehill, Haywords Heath, Sussex England, RH17 7ET.

Ecumenical Marriage. George Kilcourse, National Association of Diocesan Ecumenical Officers, Louisville, KY, 1987. Available from Office of Ecumenical Affairs, P.O. Box 942, Louisville, KY 40201.

How to Survive Being Married to a Catholic. A Redemptorist Pastoral Publication, Liguori Publications, Liguori, MO, 1985.

"Interfaith Marriage: A Special but Common Case" from *Lifelong Marriage, Is It Possible?* Creighton University Conference Proceedings, Editor Finion N. Meis, 1989. Available from the Diocesan Family Life Office, 3214 North 60th Street, Omaha, NE 68104.

Living the Faith You Share. Prepared by the Massachusetts Commission on Christian Unity, Whittemore Associates, 3 Wexford Street, Needham Heights, MA 02194.

Two Church Families. Association of Interchurch Families, The Old Bakery, Donehill, Haywords Heath, Sussex England, RH17 7ET, 1983.

6. Loss and Grief

A lot of "head stuff" about God and why this happened to our family didn't help me much. It didn't help when people tried to explain God's part in this. It didn't help my faith in God at all. What really convinced me that God cared for me were the simple things: hugs, shared tears, smiles when I needed them, a listening ear, an invitation to go out for supper, a note in the mail. That's how I experienced faith in God during my loss: from the kindness and love of others.

Bereaved mother of seven

Loss and separation are integral parts of life. The experience of loss is one of our greatest causes of stress. Learning to deal with loss and helping children deal with loss are important tasks. When that loss is death, children will need to grieve that loss and say good-bye to their loved ones, just as adults do.

Understanding the ways we respond to the experience of loss helps us deal with the losses in our own life and in the lives of our children. How we handle "little" griefs, for instance, will give us the mental and moral strength to deal with major losses. Realizing that the grief process is normal and can take a very long time is a step toward survival. Nature is a powerful ally.

Loss and Faith

Intellectually, Christians can accept and explain the death of a loved one, because they believe that when the body dies, the spirit continues to live. An anonymous quotation says, "Death is not extinguishing the light; it's putting out the lamp because the dawn has come." In the Christian family, death is an ending and a beginning.

That understanding, however, does not alleviate the wrenching pain of grief that is inevitable for us and for our children when we experience the death of someone we love. Children learn to understand the intermingling of sorrow and joy that accompanies death by watching us. However, it is difficult for us to bear in mind the importance of example-setting when we're immersed in deep grief. Most of our energy is taken up with our sense of loss and the myriad of details and practical matters that need to be arranged.

A mother of two children, eight and twelve, described it this way: "I was numb. We were into basic survival. Some days I felt like a robot. It took all my energy just to get up and have clothes ready for everyone to wear. Religion classes for my kids seemed like a luxury. Faith, God: that kind of stuff was the last thing on my mind."

The loss of his wife propelled one father into acting like a super dad. "I was propelled by what I thought were my kids needs. I learned how to do everything without her. Really, it was anger that made me get up each day and care for my kids. I was mad, mad at her and really mad at God. So, why would I — how could I — pray or talk to my kids about God?"

Another mother describes her response: "I was drowning; I knew I needed help. I trusted God would help me somehow. Some days, however, I couldn't even pray. I would just dump myself in a heap before God and cry."

Although there are predictable stages to the grieving process, each person's immediate response and movement through those stages will be different, depending on the circumstances and depth of the loss. Similarly, every person's feelings about God will be different. Some will blame God; others will find comfort and healing in the compassionate presence of people who bring the love of Jesus to them.

The tragedy of human loss has been examined, explored, explained, and expressed by artists, writers, prophets, philosophers, and psychologists — and still it is a mystery for each person who faces it.

When we're dealing with our own loss, it's difficult to deal with our children's questions about the loss itself and God's part in it. The healthiest response is to enter fully into our own grief and to allow our children the freedom to do the same. The grief process is a spiritual journey, filled with dark valleys and steep inclines. The promise we carry as Christians is that resurrection and new life awaits us at journey's end. We are guaranteed the company of Jesus, who himself suffered every loss: friends, reputation, and life.

When we stop trying to deny our children's grief or make it go away, we begin the real task of sharing faith. Our presence with our children on their grief journey is their experience of God...their simple proof of God's love and care for them in this painful time.

Understanding the
Body/Spirit Relationship

If children do not have to deal with the death of a loved one at a young age, they will learn about death gradually, just as they learn other facts of life. The death of a pet or a death portrayed on television is an opportunity for discussion. Questions about death should be answered honestly.

The parents of a five-year-old boy donated their son's organs so another child could live. They wanted to be sure that their two young daughters did not believe that their brother lived on in the other child. They used the example of a cocoon and a butterfly. They explained that their little brother had gone to heaven — just like a butterfly wiggles out of its cocoon and flits away to play in the meadow, leaving the cocoon behind.

These parents needed a concept that helped their little girls understand death and resurrection. The girls were comforted by the image of the cocoon left behind and the butterfly flying off to play in the meadow.

This concept can comfort children who have to say good-bye to a beloved grandparent. The cocoon can be old and wrinkled or stunning and beautiful; it's not the cocoon itself that's important. It's the fact that a loved one is gone to another place. The image of the cocoon and butterfly helps keep the burial of the body in perspective.

The Grief Process

Naturally, you want to protect your children from anything painful, be that something as ordinary as losing a soccer game or something extraordinary such as the death of a loved one. Whatever the loss, children will go through a grief process. When your children grieve the death of a family member, allow them to grieve in a way appropriate to their age and maturity.

Grief is an emotional wound that requires healing, not unlike a physical wound. When we lose somebody we love or something we value, we have to work through the stages of grief. Unwillingness to do so can lead to a more serious problem than the loss itself.

Family psychologist John Rosemond says that in responding to death or some other significant loss, children experience the same emotions as do adults. They simply tend to express them in slightly different ways.

Dr. Elisabeth Kubler-Ross, the author of *On Death and Dying,* says that human beings go through several stages following a loss. Though Ross's book deals with people who are coming to terms with their own terminal illness, these stages are common to all people who have to work through the loss of a loved one.

Not all people go through all stages in the same way, however. Not everyone experiences the stages in the same depth or manner. Typically, people do experience these stages in some form, and they come and go as healing progresses. Grief, most people will tell you, is a roller-coaster experience: decreasing lows and increasing highs until you reach the point where you finally accept the reality and permanence of the loss and are ready to get on with living.

Denial: The stages, as Ross describes them, begin with denial and isolation, the feeling that "this can't have happened. It can't be true." Children may escape into fantasy to cope with their pain.

Anger: For many, anger follows that initial denial. Although the anger can be overwhelming, it should be welcomed. It is a sign that the emotional wound is beginning to heal. There will be questions for which there are no answers: "Why me?" "Why now?" "Why this way?" Grief-stricken people lash out in anger because they're in so much pain. They are angry with everybody, even those closest to them. Sometimes they're especially angry at the person who died — and at God. Children will be angry at somebody or something, maybe the deceased. They need the freedom to express that anger.

Bargaining: In Ross's sequence, the third stage is the bargaining phase: where one tries to make some kind of deal with the Lord, for instance, or the doctor or even with one's own self in order to change what's happened.

Children will typically feel guilt, blaming themselves because of something they said perhaps years before. They may also try to bargain with God: "If you bring Daddy back, I'll never make him mad again." Dr. Rosemond says, "Feelings of guilt are almost inevitable when a sibling dies, because the surviving child can usually remember having wished for the sibling's death during past conflicts." Parents play an important role when they acknowledge their children's feelings and help them realize they played no role in the death.

Depression: The next phase is depression. Keep in mind that the phases don't necessarily occur in neat succession; some persons experience deep depression before they can give themselves permission to be angry. Adults and children need someone to talk to: a friend, a counselor, an understanding pastor. As they work through the pain, they may need to go over — again and again — what happened. When we are in deep grief, we need somebody to listen to us — really listen — not judge, advise, or chastise.

At this stage, persons prepare to return to normal living. These persons need to be gentle with themselves and with their children and to actively seek out people and activities that are nourishing.

With time, the grief lessens; eventually, you and your children come to some kind of acceptance. It's hard to believe this when you're in the grip of pain — but it does happen. Life will never be quite the same — but it will be good again.

Developmental Stages and the Grief Process

Children heal at their own unique pace, according to their level of development. Between the ages of three and six, children perceive death as reversible, a temporary thing. Typically, they fear separation more than death. When they experience loss, they may revert to earlier behaviors such as temper tantrums and clinging.

From six to eight, children begin to understand that death is permanent and all living things die. They still don't perceive death as personal and may think that they can escape death by their own efforts.

Between eight and twelve, children begin to perceive death as permanent — and personal. Even though they are afraid of death, children in this age group may show a fascination for the details of death.

Between the ages of twelve and seventeen, children reach adult levels of understanding about death. They may spend time thinking about death and have intense emotions about it. When adolescents lose loved ones, they need others to be particularly sensitive to those times when the deceased will be especially missed: anniversaries of the death and birthdays, for example.

As children move from concrete to abstract thinking, they may have to deal with a certain loss again, in the light of their new maturity. Some children, like some adults, deny the loss and then have to deal with it years down the road. Parents, teachers, and others who deal with these children should be sensitive to signs indicating this. Young people may begin to act out, get depressed, explode with anger, or show other signs that they are severely troubled. The children themselves may not recognize what is happening. Adults close to them are advised to be available, to listen, and to accept their feelings. Encourage these youngsters to share memories and work through their anger and pain.

Writing in the field of grief, Sandra Fox has described four tasks that grieving children need to accomplish to work through the process.

First, children need to understand. They need to accept the fact that the loss is real; it did happen.

Next, children need to grieve. They need to move through the various feelings that are part of the mourning experience.

Children also need to commemorate the death. They need to mark the death or loss in formal or informal acts, celebrations, rituals, or remembrances. Keeping alive the memory of a loved one is important to children. It's helpful to sit down with them and look at pictures or share special memories about how Grandma used to make cookies or how Grandpa used to play ball.

The final task of the child is to move on, engage in life again. Children often need permission for this. You may need to model this behavior for your children, being sensitive to their needs.

Helpful Hints

Children need to talk about their feelings when they're ready to. They will express their sense of loss in their own unique ways. Don't be surprised if the children show little emotion, even at the death of a family member. This does not mean that they're insensitive; it simply means that they're reacting as children. They cannot comprehend or deal with the full impact of the loss.

Sharing your faith at this time is an important component in the healing process. Studies show that families with a spiritual connection are stronger and happier, so it stands to reason that their faith will stand them in good stead in times of grief. Prayer is a powerful healer. Encouraging your children to pray — and praying together as a family — for your lost loved one and your own solace and peace will begin the positive process of acceptance.

Further explanations of how grief may be experienced by bereaved children are listed below. Understanding them will help you help your children.

Apparent lack of feeling: Though it may seem inappropriate, this can be a protective mechanism, nature's way of caring for children. It allows them to detach. This behavior can be a necessary step toward healing.

Regressive behavior: Children may return to behaviors that gave them comfort when they were younger. They will need attention, comfort, and acceptance without fear of judgment.

"Big man" or "little woman" syndrome: Some children attempt to grow up quickly and take the place of the person who died. Allow children to grieve in their own way. Avoid comments like "You have to be the man (woman) of the house now" to counteract this syndrome.

Explosive emotions: The most upsetting dimension of grief is a child's exploding emotion such as anger, hatred, jealousy, or terror. This behavior, upsetting for parents, is healthy. It provides a way for the child to temporarily protest the loss. Children who are not permitted to protest may turn the anger inward, resulting in depression, low self-esteem, and even physical complaints.

Acting-out behavior: Many children respond to grief by acting out. Their grades may drop, they may get into trouble, they may be unusually rude and disobedient. Children's fears and feelings provoke this kind of behavior. Try to discern the children's needs. Children who are acting out are saying "I hurt, too."

Loss and loneliness: Children suffer loss and loneliness as they struggle to come to terms with the finality of their loss. Help them through this extremely vulnerable time by showing them, in words and touch, that they are not alone. Help them move through grief toward acceptance and living fully again.

Reconciliation: Children never get over their grief; they become reconciled to it. They learn, as adults do, that life will be different, but it can be good again. Children do, eventually, come to terms with their loss.

The Healing Power of Tears

Noted music minister Deana Edwards says tears are our God-given human right. They are a great way to say "I care; I love you." Adults and children, male and female, need to recognize tears as a healing gift. To give in to the pain with tears is a human and natural response. We need to cry together as family and friends. We need to cry alone.

Tears will not come on order; we cannot force or manufacture them. But they will come. When they do, we need to let them flow. Children who are grief stricken, for instance, may cry torrents when they stub a toe or break a toy, because it allows them to give in to their grief.

Tears have cleansing and healing power. To deny your children their natural need to cry — and to hold back your own tears — is to impede a healthy experience of grieving.

Taking Children to Funerals

Alan Wolfelt, director for the Center for Loss and Life Transition, offers the following guidelines for involving children in the funeral of a friend or relative:

- Encourage children to attend the funeral, but don't make unnecessary threats. Leave the choice to them if at all possible.
- Tell the children ahead of time who will be there, how long it will last, what's expected of them, and so forth.
- Tell the children that people will be crying, and that's all right.
- Your children's first visit to the funeral home should be with people they know and with whom they're comfortable. It allows them to react and openly express feelings.
- Children need the physical closeness of parents and other caring adults before, during, and after the funeral. A hand to hold is more important than words.
- Children may not show grief at the funeral; it's their way of coping.
- Be especially patient and empathetic at this time.

Children can also be allowed to have some part in the burial itself, as in the death of a father of eleven and grandfather of twenty-nine. All the children and grandchildren wrote messages on the plain wooden casket. In another family, each grandchild took a flower from the bouquet on the casket to press and keep to honor their grandfather's memories.

When a Mass is celebrated for a deceased family member, some families attend as a group, grieve their loss, and pray for strength. Some families make special trips to the cemetery after the funeral to reminisce and say special good-byes. These activities are cathartic and give the message to young people that it's okay to grieve, it's okay to cry. After all, Jesus wept.

Help your children understand that death is universal and inevitable. Tell them the truth; do not tell them things that are misleading or confusing. Comments like "Grandpa is just sleeping" or "God wanted Grandpa to come home" can lead to a fear of sleep and a bitterness toward God.

Ask for Help

Healing does not progress in a straight line. It has dramatic leaps and depressing backslides. Understanding that, you can take comfort in the knowledge that the grief process is underway. If you or your children seem to be hitting rock bottom, seek professional help. It's not only okay, it's essential. It's okay to feel anger and depression; it's not okay to be destructive or to hate oneself.

Rainbows for All God's Children is a support-group program for children and youth who have experienced death or divorce in their families. It is offered through schools and religious-education programs throughout this country. Another group in the Church that addresses the experience of death and divorce is the Beginning Experience ministry for adults. You may find this especially helpful for yourself in the process of moving on with life. A special weekend called Young Adult Beginning Experience (YABE) for youngsters age sixteen to twenty-five-plus is also offered through the diocesan office of youth ministry and family-life office. If there is no local program available, you may call the national office for information. That address and others are in the resource listing on page 136.

Christians can work through these experiences in the company of others whose faith is founded on Jesus Christ. This faith recognizes that death has no power over us, nor does loss of any kind. Those who follow Jesus know, even when they cannot feel it, that resurrection follows for all those who place their grief in the lap of God's mercy and compassion.

Resources

Child's View of Grief, Alan Wolfelt, Center for Loss and Life Transition, 3735 Broken Bow Road, Fort Collins, CO 80526, 1991. (Twenty-minute video also available.)

Explaining Death to Children. Earl A. Grollman, ed., Beacon Press, Boston, 1969.

Fall of Freddie the Leaf, The. Leo F. Buscaglia, Slack Inc., Thorofare, NJ, 1982.

On Children and Death. Elisabeth Kubler-Ross, Macmillan, New York, 1985.

On Death and Dying. Elisabeth Kubler-Ross, Macmillan, New York, 1970.

Windows, Healing, and Helping Through Loss. Mary Jo Hannaford and Michael Popkin, Active Parenting, Inc., Marietta, GA, 1991. (Video with leader's guide and participant's workbook.)

Additional Sources of Information

Beginning Experience, Central Office, 305 Michigan Avenue, Detroit, MI 48226.

National Catholic Ministry to the Bereaved, 7835 Harvard Avenue, Cleveland, OH 44105.

North American Conference of Separated and Divorced Catholics (NACSDC), 1100 South Goodman Street, Rochester, NY 14620.

Rainbows for All God's Children, National Office, 1111 Tower Road, Schaumburg, IL 68073.

7. Sexuality

Sexuality education, which is the basic right and duty of parents, must always be carried out under their attentive guidance whether at home or in education centers....

John Paul II
*Apostolic Exhortation
on the Family* (#37)

Never has there been a more important time for parents to turn their minds to appropriate sexuality education for their children than there is now. Sex, it would seem, has become nothing but an indoor/outdoor sport in the world at large, and children are overwhelmed with confusing messages. Many parents, however, find it awkward to share information about sex, especially with children who are in stages where sharing anything can be a challenge.

By the time our children enter first grade, they have had a broad range of sexual experiences and volumes of information about sex.

The experiences start at birth with the soft and loving touch of a parent. Children receive a myriad of sexuality messages from relatives, friends, TV, and parental attitudes toward potty-training experiences, play activity, clothing, and so forth.

Parents, as the primary educators of children, must compete with inappropriate external information: "Everyone has a right to free sex," "Anything is acceptable between consenting adults," "If you are not sexually active, there must be something wrong with you." Sexual activity is treated as a private matter, a personal decision, with no regard for its social, spiritual, or psychological consequences. All these messages contradict what our children hear and see us convey at home.

Most activities and discussions in the media are about sex as a genital activity, not about human sexuality as a key element of the human personality.

Integrated Sexuality

We are sexual beings. We cannot separate our sexuality from the mainstream of life and treat it as a separate entity. Healthy sexuality is integrated into the whole fabric of our lives.

When we educate our children in human sexuality, we are doing more than explaining the functions of body parts. The Catholic Christian tradition regards sexuality as a "fundamental component of personality, of manifestation, of communication with others, of feeling, of expressing and of living human love" *(Educational Guidance in Human Love)*.

Our sexual dimension is at the heart of the Christian tradition's mandate to love one another. Flowing out of our sexuality is our ability to understand others, to be sensitive, to be intimate, to have compassion for others, and to be open and mutually supportive.

Human sexuality draws us to others, to personal commitment, and to love. We relate to God and to each other as male or female.

So, teaching our children about genital sexual activity is only one dimension of the good news of human sexuality.

The most important lesson we teach about human sexuality will be in the way we express love — to those in the home and in the world. Faithful and committed love, care for one's spouse and one's children, treating one another with appropriate affection and respect, treating sexuality with reverence and respect: these are the makings of our children's healthy sexuality education.

Much of what children learn about sexuality is learned indirectly while concentrating on healthy personal development in the grade-school years. Children who are raised in this positive atmosphere have self-esteem and learn to make mature decisions. They develop self-discipline and learn control of their urges and actions; they learn how to express affection in healthy ways; they develop good communication skills. They have a genuine appreciation of what it means to be male or female.

Our day-to-day relationships may not seem, on the surface, to be "sex" information. But these are the skills and attitudes upon which a child's sexual maturity is built. Without them, knowledge about genital sexual activity cannot bring happiness.

Why Parents Remain Silent

Why do so many parents remain silent or timidly quiet in the face of all the unhealthy information that surrounds their children? Often it's because they just don't know how to talk about it. The parents themselves sometimes feel that they did not receive adequate information from their parents, and still — they think — "everything turned out all right."

That won't wash in the sexually permissive and pluralistic society of today. Parents cannot afford to be silent, particularly if they are believing Christians.

Parents may also be silent because they naively think their children know what they need to know about sexuality. They also may believe their religion teachers "go over it" in class. Children are being educated all right, but not the way parents think. Children are exposed to at least three to five hours of sex education every day — much of it inappropriate. Children are a valuable market for advertisers who use sex to sell products.

Some parents are timid because of their own uncertainty about their personal sexual values and beliefs. Lack of parental conviction on issues such as equality of the sexes, intimacy and commitment, sexual intercourse, pornography, abortion, masturbation, homosexuality, and a host of other issues can lead to a deadly silence that children may hear as agreement with society's point of view.

For some parents, silence on sexual matters may result in confusion about the Church's teaching. They may know the Church's teaching on birth control and abortion — but that's not the full teaching on sexuality that the Church offers. They may see the Church as restrictive, living in the Dark Ages, and not a real authority on matters of sex.

A parent's responsibility for passing on sexual values is supported by the Church's teaching and shared by the Christian community who hold and protect a rich tradition of the "good news" about sexuality.

The Good News

Sex is good; sex is sacred. The Church teaches that sex is creative and life-giving. Like all human powers, sexuality is a gift given by God for human happiness, a vehicle for knowing and experiencing God. Human happiness is a result of using these gifts appropriately. As parents, we need not apologize for or even speak timidly about this positive vision.

Sexual expressions and sexual intercourse are expressions of lifelong commitment and covenant love and are intended for marriage. This is the Church's teaching. In view of the abject failure of the sexual revolution, the Church's teaching is now being recognized as the ultimate in common sense. That teaching encourages chastity for all Christians — single, married, ordained, or religious.

Pope Paul VI's encyclical *Humanae Vitae (Of Human Life)* put forth a whole vision of human sexuality. Most people have no grasp of this document beyond the Church's teaching on birth control. Yet, the encyclical describes the dignity of all human life and the responsibility that comes with being a sexual being in a world that seriously questions that dignity. It affirms the value of human life and the goodness of sexuality. That is the message we can pass on with confidence to our children.

Stages of Development and Sexuality

It is important to take a child's stage of development into consideration when passing on sexual values. Sexuality is an integral part of a child's personality and is central to a healthy understanding of self as male or female. It is a critical factor in a child's relationship with others.

Children between the ages of seven and nine will be interested in the distinctions between male and female. This is a good time to affirm your children's unique maleness or femaleness while avoiding sexual stereotypes. It is helpful for children in single-parent families who do not have a male or female role model to adopt such a model with whom they can identify and share experiences. Children of this age develop an increasing responsibility toward themselves and learn the consequences of behaviors. Therein lies the foundation for control and responsible use of slowly blossoming sexual powers.

By ten or eleven, some children will begin puberty, with a strong need to conform to peer expectations. When children don't measure up to their peers' or the media's standards for maleness or femaleness, their self-esteem may need serious boosting from supportive parents.

The intermediate years are characterized by intellectual curiosity and an interest in new facts about everything. This is a key teaching curiosity — a teachable moment — before full adolescence begins. Your children will still listen openly to you; talk with your children about sex. If using books or tapes or going to programs makes it easier for you, the resource listing on pages 144-145 offers suggestions.

Whatever method you use, parental discussion is very effective at this stage. Children feel privileged to have parents talk with them about grown-up matters. There will be teachable moments available to you that will not be available when the inwardness and awkwardness of thirteen appears.

By the time children reach the age of twelve or thirteen, their insecurities and drive for separateness may make it difficult to communicate with them. At this age, however, their increased ability to think abstractly and question beliefs and behaviors create opportunities for offering additional information about the meaning and limitations of sexuality. Their exposure in the media's handling of pornography, abortion, sexual abuse, and deviant behavior will create some confusion; they will have questions.

As your children approach adolescence, set clear limits on sexual experimentation and involvement. Catholic teaching provides these limits based on an understanding of the meaning of human sexuality and our destiny as God's beloved creation. Children of this age have great concerns about their own sexual thoughts and feelings and may experience anxiety and confusion about what is normal. If you're uncomfortable discussing these matters with your children, and many parents are, you will find help in the resource listing on pages 144-145. You may want to ask your children to read a chapter or section of a book that deals with a difficult issue and then ask them a few questions about what they read. If they communicate, thank the Lord and go on from there. If they don't, thank the Lord anyway and realize that you have at least made the information available to them.

Sharing your own convictions and principles is the most effective way of passing on sexual values. Do not remain silent on this crucial subject! Emphasize the positive power and beauty of sexuality at every stage and discuss its meaning for marriage and family.

The purpose of passing on sexual values is not to create feelings of guilt and shame in children and young adolescents. It is to give your children an understanding of their own beautiful and powerful sexuality; it is to communicate the limitations required so they will reach full sexual potential as a mature and confident adult.

Helpful Hints

Parents most frequently ask, "How and when should I approach sexual issues?" Here are five suggestions that have worked for many parents.

Look for teachable moments. The birth of a child, a news story on date rape, the onset of wet dreams or menstruation, a classroom biology unit on reproduction, or a neighbor's or family member's pregnancy before marriage are all teachable moments. Remember: these are *teachable* moments, not *preachable* moments. Talk about your own Christian values and the real-life compromises of personal choices about sex.

Plan heart-to-heart talks along the way. Take time to be alone with your children. They are delighted to have one-on-one time with their parents. Special moments together are helpful in letting your children know your loving concern and how important you think this issue is.

Give a good example. Show appreciation and respect for masculine and feminine. Magazines, pictures, movies, and the language in your home all speak loudly to children about sex. Appropriate expressions of affection between parents and children are important parts of a child's sexual education.

Help your children develop life skills. Children's healthy self-esteem and communication skills will be reflected in their ability to make informed decisions, control personal urges, and resist peer pressure. Because sex is a fundamental component of personality, all these personal skills contribute to sexual maturity.

Expose the lie. Make sure your children know where you stand in regard to the media's and society's views on sexuality. Recreational or manipulative sex and viewing persons as sex objects are attitudes that lie to our children about the meaning of their sexuality. Reinforce the Church's eminently sensible teaching.

Even the people who originally touted "free love" are beginning to admit the havoc it causes in the lives of many. Young people who have been conned into thinking that sexual intercourse means love have been debased and demoralized; the results have been disastrous. Sexually transmitted diseases and the growing incidence of juvenile pregnancy are examples of this tragedy.

Sharing the truth and your personal views and experiences is the most effective way of getting these facts into the heads of your children. Labeling pornography or movies and magazines about violence and sex as "adult" gives the message that to misuse sexual power is okay when you grow up. Be clear about what is — and is not — healthy, fully human, and moral for young people and adults.

Books, tapes, and programs to help you with these issues may be available through your church or diocesan family-life or youth offices.

Good News for Everyone

If you have more than one child, you will be sharing sexual information and values at several levels simultaneously. Following the basic Christian beliefs about sexuality will apply to every stage of growth and can be shared with your child in ordinary ways every day. The following messages apply to all children (and all adults).

You are a unique creation. You are made in God's image. You have special talents and gifts. You are a wonderful creation!

You are fundamentally good, even if you do wrong sometimes. You were designed by God. Your body, your ability to love, think, run, imagine, laugh, and work, and your sexuality are good in themselves.

You are loved unconditionally by God. You were born with your own special capacity to love.

You are sexual and made of flesh and blood — and that is good. You bring that with you into every relationship. Sexuality, even though it might make you uncomfortable at times, is a gift from God.

Your sexuality is a responsibility. It can give you great pleasure if used responsibly and great pain if misused. As you discover your sexual potential and learn your limitations, be assured of the Lord's understanding. After all, it's God's gift. If you choose Christian marriage, your sexual commitment to another person is meant to unite you forever and bring new life to the larger community. A lifelong commitment means it is important to choose wisely.

These suggestions are important foundations upon which to build your children's sexuality education in the grade-school years. Your children's emerging sexual development in these years may stimulate your own growth in sexuality and an appreciation for the Church's teachings.

Resources

Apostolic Exhortation on the Family (Familiaris Consortio). John Paul II, 1981. (Order from the United States Catholic Conference, 3211 Fourth Street, NE, Washington, DC 20017-1194.)

Becoming a Man, Basic Information, Guidance, and Attitudes on Sex for Boys. William J. Bausch, Twenty-Third Publications, Mystic, CT, 1988.

Becoming a Woman, Basic Information, Guidance, and Attitudes on Sex for Girls. Valerie R. Dillon, Twenty-Third Publications, Mystic, CT, 1990.

Educational Guidance in Human Love: Outlines for Sex Education. Sacred Congregation for Catholic Education, United States Catholic Conference, 3211 Fourth Street, NE, Washington, DC 20017-1194, 1981.

Human Sexuality: A Catholic Perspective for Education and Lifelong Learning. United States Catholic Conference, 3211 Fourth Street, NE, Washington, DC 20017-1194, 1991.

Love, Sex, and God (Sex Education Series). Bill Ameiss and Jane Graver, Concordia, St. Louis, 1986.

Parents Talk Love. Susan K. Sullivan and Matthew A. Kawaik, Bantam, New York, 1988.

Sex Education for Toddlers to Young Adults: A Guide for Parents. James Kenny, St. Anthony Messenger Press, Cincinnati, 1990.

8. The Media

Because television makes so much accessible to children that was not accessible to them before, it hurries children to grow up fast. Young children today can experience events through television that, given other media, they could not experience until a later age.

David Elkind
The Hurried Child

In a school cafeteria line, in a space of ten minutes, you can observe grade-school children wearing a wide variety of television heroes on their T-shirts and sweatshirts. They sport slogans, scenes, and characters from countless cartoon programs, sitcoms, and the newest rock group.

This is an electronic plugged-in generation. Most grade-school children spend four to seven hours a day viewing television or playing video games. TV-watching increases in grade-school years, peaks in the early teens, and falls off in adolescence when teenagers become more involved outside the home.

Studies show that children have spent more time watching TV than they have spent in school by the time they reach age eighteen.

This is a good-news/bad-news situation. At best, television brings world-changing events, educational programs, plays, operas, major athletic events, and the most recent scientific discoveries right into our living rooms. For a few dollars, you can take a whole birthday party to see a recent box-office hit — right in your own living room.

On the other hand, recent studies have documented alarming facts about television viewing. It discourages reading and stifles creativity. It encourages passivity and is an obstacle to the development of social skills. It glorifies violence, which tends to make children more aggressive. It encourages sexual and racial stereotypes and uses up valuable free time that children might otherwise use to enhance their physical, social, and intellectual growth. That's bad news.

Making Television a Positive Influence

The difficult task of determining whether television will have a negative or positive influence on children will fall, primarily, to parents. Who else? The grade-school years is the time for parents to decide what action they will take to determine that TV will be a positive influence on their children.

Children between the ages of eight and ten are in a transition of cognitive growth. They need help in developing reasoning and logical-thinking skills. With parental assistance and guidance, television can help that development.

The intermediate-age child is especially vulnerable and susceptible to influences in the media. Children's reading skills are refined and sharpened in these years, and too much television can rob them of the needed time to develop these skills. Early adolescents, who may be testing faith and family values, view television personalities and heroes with a naiveté that might be harmful.

You may wonder what TV has to do with sharing faith with your child. Parents who have wrestled with this question offer this comment: "If we are going to consciously and consistently try to build a strong family life and share faith with one another in our homes, we will have to decide how we use our time together and what kind of influences we allow to enter our home. Television can be used to bring us together and encourage learning and sharing. It can also stymie communication and alienate us from one another. It can bring into our home enriching experiences — or it can bring negative influences that belittle and contradict Christian values."

Helpful Hints

Resources and classes are available to help parents who want more information on how to manage television wisely. The following suggestions are taken from those resources. They can contribute to creating a faith atmosphere in your home.

Set time limits. Teach children to balance TV with active participation in sports, hobbies, reading, chores, and other healthy activities. No more than two hours a day is recommended for grade-school children. Many parents stipulate the time for television: not after eight-thirty in the evening, not at mealtime, not until homework is finished. Watching television during family meals discourages communication and diminishes the small amount of time families have together.

Provide guidelines. Consult the TV section of your local newspaper and post it on your set, highlighting the programs children may choose to watch. As your children reach early adolescence, they should have more say in the choices. Random searching for shows increases arguments between siblings and presents young children with choices that are sometimes unhealthy or inappropriate for their age level.

Avoid using the TV as background noise in your home. It encourages children to watch programs they do not consciously choose and stifles creativity in using free time. Studies show that the content of programs children watch makes a substantial difference in their overall development. If these guidelines are set for children in preschool years, they are easier to enforce in later years.

It is never too late, however, to make a change that will positively affect your children's TV-viewing habits. If you are starting with older children, the first few weeks will be difficult, and it will take courage to remain firm. You may want to offer incentives and suggest alternative activities. The payoff is big dividends in your children's development and in the time the family has to relate to one another.

Watch television with your child. Talk with your children about what they liked best and what they liked least. Ask them to compare situations on TV with their own experiences. As children enter early adolescence, some flexibility with rules will be necessary, but children should always be given clear standards about what is acceptable in your home and what is not.

Encourage a balance. The amount of time you allow your children to spend in front of a TV screen should include news, documentaries, educational specials, comedy, good drama, appropriate "junk" TV, and interactive TV games. Expose your children to the rich variety of peoples, cultures, and programs that will enrich their faith. When significant TV ministries are presented, one family spreads a blanket and has a picnic supper in the family room so they can experience the program together. Viewed in this way, TV can nourish both children and adults.

Examine your own television viewing habits. Children can learn — by noting your own TV-viewing habits — that TV can be used to escape duties or relationships. If watching sporting events, for example, is consistently chosen over reading to children, playing games, or socializing with family and friends, children will imitate that behavior.

Often, parents don't consciously choose TV; it's just always on, and therefore a constant distraction. When you do not make conscious choices about television, then it's in control. If this is the case at your house and you want to make changes, some of the recommended reading in the resource listing on page 150 may be helpful. Changing viewing habits is not easy, but the rewards are significant.

Learn about television programming and its effects. The resource listing also mentions magazines, weekly review services, and books that assist parents in knowing the content of television and video programming. Weekly papers, including your Catholic weekly publication, often review television programs in advance. These equip you to make a choice about what you and your family watch. If nothing is available locally, an annual subscription to a media magazine would be of help.

Talk back to television. Viewers are powerful in the land of television advertising. If you like something, let stations, producers, and advertisers know. If you find programs or advertisements distasteful or inappropriate, speak up! There's no group more powerful than outraged parents complaining, not to one another, but to the sponsoring network. Support the groups who fight this insidious problem. Organized national and local groups can make a difference.

Provide alternatives. Many parents are too busy, too tired, or too lazy to create positive alternatives for themselves or their children's leisure time. What's more, television can become addictive, and not an easy habit to change. In a book called *What to Do After You Turn Off the TV,* Frances Moore Lappe gives imaginative and practical ideas to parents who may be too young to recall what children and families did before television. One young family had so much fun playing together when the electricity went off for a weekend that they never did return to their compulsive TV-watching habits.

What comes into your home through the television screen can enrich and strengthen your family's growth and faith or diminish it.

The choice is yours.

Resources

Hurried Child: Growing Up Too Fast Too Soon. David Elkind, Addison-Wesley, Redding, MA, 1988.

Media and Values. A quarterly review of media issues and trends, 1962 South Shenandoah, Los Angeles, CA 19934.

TV and Movie Guide. Weekly newsletter previewing upcoming network TV programs, video releases, and movies. Order from Catholic News Service, 3211 Fourth Street, NE, Washington, DC 20017-1100.

Unplugging the Plug-In Drug. Marie Winn, Viking Penguin, New York, 1987.

What to Do After You Turn Off the TV: Fresh Ideas for Enjoying Family Time. Frances M. Lappe, Ballantine Books, New York, 1985.

9. Your Child and Social Ills

- *Jimmy kicked Pete because Pete called him a name. You get a call from the teacher because this repeated pattern of behavior is disturbing on the playground and in the classroom.*
- *Beth approaches you the first week of December with a twenty-three item list of "Christmas hints." She has spent weeks paging through the catalogs.*
- *Terry calls his female junior-high classmates "chicks." He picked up the substitute term at school.*
- *You find an R-rated movie tucked under a stack of magazines in the family room.*
- *A parent sitting next to you on the bleachers cautions you to keep your child away from the new black football player who may be a bad influence.*
- *Your fourteen-year-old points out that the "bums" are getting a lot of news coverage because of the cold weather.*
- *Ten-year-old Sean cheers as he watches fighter pilots bombing large urban areas of enemy territory on news coverage of an international conflict.*

"Can this be my kid?" At one time or another, every parent asks this question.

The way children treat others, what they value, and their attitudes toward others are shaped by a variety of factors, the most important one being family. Social ills of sexism, racism, ageism, materialism, and violence, however, are woven into the fabric of the environment so that no child — or parent, for that matter — is untouched.

On Their Way to Adulthood

Sharing faith with our children in this culture often means teaching them to live counterculturally, which is hard to do. We want our children to be socially acceptable, successful, smart, and rich enough to have a comfortable life. We want them to have enough status to gain respect from others. On their way to gaining these good things in life, however, our children often develop attitudes and behavior that conflict with being a follower of Christ.

Jesus' main purpose was to "bring glad tidings to the poor... liberty to captives and recovery of sight to the blind" (Luke 4:18). Jesus did this in simple ordinary ways, always teaching about the infinite value and equality of all persons (the blind, tax collectors, outcasts) as brothers and sisters of the same creator God. His followers are to do likewise.

For hundreds of years, the Catholic Church has tried to champion the rights of outcasts and address the needs of the poor. The first hospitals, asylums, and schools were all started by religious men and women following the mandate of Christ.

The Church as a human institution has not been untouched by social evils. Yet, in the last one hundred years in particular, Catholic leaders have made great efforts at teaching the basics of how to treat other people. These Catholic social teachings are great helps to parents raising children in a society that often condones violence, encourages consumerism, and values things over persons.

Catholic Social Teaching

Social teaching is exactly what the words say: teaching ways to socialize, to relate to people. Both the Old and New Testaments emphasize the importance of relationships between people. In the Old Testament, over two-thirds of the religious laws had to do with how to treat persons you live with. In the New Testament, Jesus continually pointed out that the law of love for God and neighbor came before religious ritual and practices. Catholic social teaching is based on this solid scriptural foundation and has been built on the wisdom gained in human behavior throughout all of history.

The teachings of the Church have changed over the years in response to human progress and the social evils that have accompanied it. When the Industrial Revolution placed workers at risk for the sake of profit, Pope Leo XIII defended their rights as human persons in the famous encyclical *Rerum Novarum (On Capital and Labor)*, 1891. When the nuclear arms race escalated, endangering all human life and the life of the earth, Pope John XXIII spoke in *Pacem in Terris (Peace on Earth)*, 1963. American bishops have championed the rights of the economically depressed and the minorities in their recent letters. They have challenged the whole nation to recognize the equality and dignity of every human person.

Central Themes

Although specific social teachings change with the time and with human situations, there are consistent themes central to all the Church's social teachings. These themes address the social evils of our own day and provide inspiration and direction for us in raising children to be followers of Jesus Christ. The following is a summary of those themes and simple suggestions from parents for sharing these important gospel values at home with children.

Reverence for life and dignity of human persons: Human persons are made in the image and likeness of God. Each person's dignity comes not from possessions or bloodline or position, but from the very simple fact that God dwells in each person, and each person is a unique creation of God.

To convey this important gospel value to your children, avoid using slang terms for people of color or for women, and discourage your children from picking up this language from peers. When TV portrays stereotypes of ethnic groups or older persons, talk to your children about what prejudice means.

Openly support or become involved with groups who advocate for the life of the unborn, the criminals on death row, or people who are disabled or handicapped in any way.

Teach your children to resolve differences peacefully, without violence.

Balance competitive activities with cooperative activities. Teach your children that competition is necessary and good, but the ability to cooperate is more important in getting along with others.

Recognition of the rights and responsibilities of all human persons: The sacred dimension of every person makes all people equal before God. Each of us has the same human rights: the right to life and to all the basics that a full human life demands (food, clothing, shelter, education, and healthcare). Each of us has a responsibility to ourselves, our family, and to the larger community. This includes the responsibility to respect and defend others' rights and to work for the common good.

To convey this important gospel value to your children, treat your sons and daughters with equal dignity. Avoid stereotypes and degrading name-calling. Stress the importance of the unique differences of the sexes — and emphasize the equality in responsibilities, privileges, and opportunities.

Limit your use of the earth's resources in your home. Conserve energy, recycle, and limit consumption. Fast from certain things during Lent and Advent to share the earth's resources with others.

Teach your children, by your own word and deed, that social action (things you do to protect and serve others and the earth) is a faith and family activity, not simply humanitarian social service.

As a family, save clothing and collect food items for local pantries and shelters that serve the poor and homeless. Help children see that every child, no matter what color or economic level, has a right to a healthy meal and a place to sleep.

Community: Every individual is called to community. We are social beings, and we enjoy our rights and fulfill our responsibilities in relationship to other persons. The family is the first and primary community to which we are connected and responsible. It is, as we have said before, the "first church," the basic cell of society. Next to family, each person is called to participate in the larger human community, to contribute his or her gifts, to fulfill responsibilities that come with membership in neighborhood, church, city, and country.

To convey this important gospel value to your children, make family time a priority. Assign tasks that each member of the family does for the common good of everyone. Plan having fun together, working jointly on special tasks, and worshiping together.

Hold family meetings to aid in making decisions together and taking responsibility for one another's needs. Make sure children know and understand what the "common good" means.

Contribute time and energy to your neighborhood association, parish community, or civic organization. Include your children in your volunteer efforts.

While stressing your children's individual uniqueness, help them see how they are connected with other children and families because of their faith.

The dignity of work and the rights of people who work: Work is not just a way of making money; work is a way for each of us to take part in God's ongoing creative action in the world. In the Church's teachings on economic justice, the economy is always seen as a means of serving persons in their growth and development, not enslaving them for the purpose of acquiring material goods.

To convey this important gospel value to your children, provide them with opportunities to work at home and to experience how they feel differently depending on the job they're doing.

Treat all workers with respect, regardless of the job they perform. Help children see the value of whatever service others provide for you. Avoid making derogatory remarks about persons because of the work they do.

Point out to your children that some people (such as parents who scrub floors, toilets, and do the laundry) do the work because it needs to be done — and because they love the family. There is no pay for doing these jobs. These labors of love shape us into the persons we are. Also, some people work at jobs they don't necessarily like because of the need to put food on their tables. That alone can give dignity to a job.

The option for the poor and vulnerable: Persons who are poor or in need of help for any reason are regarded as first in the kingdom of God. Jesus emphasized the beloved status of the *anawin* (the poor and outcast) and challenged us to care for them.

To convey this important gospel value to your children, provide opportunities for them to see and experience how others live — especially those who have very little.

Avoid making general statements about all poor or homeless persons, refugees, or migrant workers.

Teach your children the economic and social reasons for poverty. Involve your family in service to the poor, to meet the poor as fellow human beings, not people who need help.

Simplify your lifestyle by cutting down on Christmas spending, vacation costs, or fast food, and give the extra money to a specific family who is underemployed or struggling financially for some other reason.

The one human family: We are all sisters and brothers of the one God who gives us life. Because of this spiritual connection, we are one another's keepers. That includes everyone who occupies this planet. Most Catholics learned this traditional teaching as children under the description of the "mystical Body of Christ." Today, we use the word *solidarity* to describe our intimate connection with one another in Christ.

To convey this important gospel value to your children, educate them — without scaring them — about the realities of war. Help them understand what happens to families when the destruction of war occurs.

Enjoy the foods, art, and music of other cultures in your home. Read books and watch television specials that describe the rich variety of people who occupy this planet.

Avoid jokes, cartoons, and other sources of humor that poke fun at minorities or ethnic groups.

Look for toys and books that are inclusive of children of color.

Encourage your children to have a rainbow of friends: children with disabilities and different social and faith backgrounds. Extend hospitality to those who are different from yourself.

Passing on faith and Christian values is done in our homes, in conversations with our children, and in our everyday activities. For most parents, believing in these values is not a difficult task. The challenge is living them out in relationships with others. For many of us, an ongoing change of heart is necessary if we are to pass on these values by our words and actions.

Becoming familiar with Church teaching will help. There are also many practical resources mentioned at the end of this section. These will assist you in helping your children create a just and peaceful home and world.

Many parishes have social-ministry committees that educate people and take positive action to change conditions of poverty and injustice. Join with other parents in groups such as the Parenting for Peace and Justice Network that exist in many communities.

Involve yourself and your children in the dimension of the Church's social teaching that seems right for you. No one has to do it all. If we have a desire to overcome the social evils of the world, God will usually show the way. The goal of Christian living is not perfection but consistent effort.

At the heart of the social gospel is a deep love and respect for others. Children can only love and respect others if they are treated with love and respect. Children who do not appreciate their own intrinsic value as God's unique creations cannot and will not value other persons, their work, their property, or their rights. You lay a solid foundation for Christ's social teachings by building healthy self-esteem in your children. The skills children need for life — decision-making skills, communication skills, assertiveness, and self-discipline — are all necessary traits for Christian living.

"Our faith calls us to work for justice, to serve those in need, to pursue peace, and to defend the life, dignity and rights of all our brothers and sisters. This is the call of Jesus, the challenge of the prophets and the living tradition of our church" *(A Century of Social Teaching,* U.S. Catholic Conference, November, 1990).

Resources

Building Shalom Families (VHS tape and guidebook), James McGinnis and Kathleen McGinnis, Institute for Peace and Justice, 4144 Lindell Boulevard, #400, St. Louis, MO 63100, 1980.

Century of Social Teaching: A Common Heritage, a Continuing Challenge. United States Catholic Conference, 3211 Fourth Street, NE, Washington, DC 20017-1194, November 1990.

Helping Kids Care: Harmony-Building Activities for Home, Church, and School. Camy Condon and James McGinnis, Meyer Stone Books, New York, 1988.

Parenting for Peace and Justice Newsletter. The Institute for Peace and Justice, 4144 Lindell Boulevard, #400, St. Louis, MO 63100.

Parenting for Peace and Justice, Ten Years Later. James McGinnis and Kathleen McGinnis, Orbis Books, Maryknoll, NY, 1982.

Shaping a New World. NETWORK, a National Catholic Social Justice Lobby, Washington, DC 20018, 1991.

Starting Out Right, Nurturing Your Children as Peacemakers. Kathleen McGinnis and Barbara Oehlberg, Meyer Stone Books, New York, and the Institute for Peace and Justice, 4144 Lindell Boulevard, #400, St. Louis, MO 63100, 1988.

Way to Peace: Liberation Through the Bible. John Topel, Orbis Books, Maryknoll, NY, 1979.

A Final Word

We hope this book has affirmed the many ways you are already sharing the Catholic faith with your child. We hope you've gleaned some new ideas and feel encouraged to seek out further resources.

Individual parents, extended families, and whole faith communities are most effective when they join together to support the faith of children. The following personal stories illustrate the importance of this cooperation in nurturing the spiritual life of children, from generation to generation in the domestic church.

* * *

My husband, Kip, and I have six children who have become wonderful human beings (my own assessment). We live on a farm, feed cattle, and have endured the rags to riches and back again economy that afflicts farmers and ranchers. When our children were young, even when we couldn't possibly afford it, Kip and I would go off to the city — about sixty miles away — and have a night out. We'd go to a movie or just have a nice meal. We'd communicate.

In retrospect, we believe those "nights out" were the most important thing we did for our relationship. It is so easy to lose track of each other in the turbulence of raising a family — to wake up when the children are all gone and wonder who that is sitting across the breakfast table from you. We nurtured each other, our relationship, and thus our family.

Joan Burney

* * *

My grandmother's faith was a "faith generator" for all of us. She had three small shrines on her kitchen cabinet. Oil-and-water vigil lights blazed in front of each of them when a neighbor was sick, money was in short supply, or a family member was traveling a long distance. On her nightstand lay an old tattered book of prayers. She usually said them in private.

From my childhood, I remember long walks to church on the Fridays of Lent for the stations and trips to clean the church before Christmas. Grandma sang lullabies to us in the rocking chair about how God loved us and how the saints were our protection against evil. Her favorites were Saint Anthony, Saint Joseph, and the Virgin Mary. Most religious rules and regulations were assumed behavior in our home except when special circumstances called for a suspension for certain individuals.

We were taken to church for weekly Mass and monthly confession. Huge parties with favorite foods and heaps of affirmation for honored guests were regularly planned for baptisms, first Communions, confirmations, graduations, weddings, and funerals. Grandma would gently pinch the cheeks of every child and grandchild and proclaim their beauty, talent, or intelligence, and their beloved status to all.

Grandma didn't have much formal religious education, but the depth of her faith, the warmth and love in her home, and the way she treated us in ordinary things were faith experiences for me.

Mary Jo Pedersen